Next.js Quick Start Guide

Server-side rendering done right

Kirill Konshin

BIRMINGHAM - MUMBAI

Next.js Quick Start Guide

Commissioning Editor: Amarabha Banerjee
Acquisition Editor: Reshma Raman
Content Development Editor: Roshan Kumar
Technical Editor: Shweta Jadhav
Copy Editor: Safis Editing
Project Coordinator: Hardik Bhinde
Proofreader: Safis Editing
Indexer: Priyanka Dhadke
Graphics: Jason Monteiro
Production Coordinator: Arvindkumar Gupta

First published: July 2018

Production reference: 1230718

Published by Packt Publishing Ltd.
Livery Place
35 Livery Street
Birmingham
B3 2PB, UK.

ISBN 978-1-78899-366-1

www.packtpub.com

To my parents, family, and to all friends for their love and support.

– Kirill Konshin

mapt.io

Mapt is an online digital library that gives you full access to over 5,000 books and videos, as well as industry leading tools to help you plan your personal development and advance your career. For more information, please visit our website.

Why subscribe?

- Spend less time learning and more time coding with practical eBooks and Videos from over 4,000 industry professionals
- Improve your learning with Skill Plans built especially for you
- Get a free eBook or video every month
- Mapt is fully searchable
- Copy and paste, print, and bookmark content

PacktPub.com

Did you know that Packt offers eBook versions of every book published, with PDF and ePub files available? You can upgrade to the eBook version at www.PacktPub.com and as a print book customer, you are entitled to a discount on the eBook copy. Get in touch with us at service@packtpub.com for more details.

At www.PacktPub.com, you can also read a collection of free technical articles, sign up for a range of free newsletters, and receive exclusive discounts and offers on Packt books and eBooks.

Contributors

About the author

Kirill Konshin is the principal software developer at RingCentral, the world's leading Cloud communications provider. He is a highly experienced professional in full-stack web engineering with more than 10 years of experience, proficient in all the most recent web technologies. He is also an active open source contributor to React-related projects. You can follow him on Medium.

About the reviewer

Chris van Rensburg has been involved in JavaScript since the very birth of the language from its early progenitor, LiveScript, that was developed in the 90s by Netscape. While then working for a small start-up in San Mateo, Chris was part of a pitch to Netscape executives on how web pages could be made interactive by the addition of event handler attributes to HTML tags for invoking actions. Chris went on to develop high-level JavaScript frameworks, culminating in the UIZE JavaScript Framework.

Packt is searching for authors like you

If you're interested in becoming an author for Packt, please visit `authors.packtpub.com` and apply today. We have worked with thousands of developers and tech professionals, just like you, to help them share their insight with the global tech community. You can make a general application, apply for a specific hot topic that we are recruiting an author for, or submit your own idea.

Table of Contents

Preface

This book guides developers from building simple, single-page applications to fully-fledged, scalable, and reliable client-server infrastructures that enable code sharing between client and server, universal modules, and server-side rendering. This book explains the best practices for building sites using Next.js, enabling readers to build SEO-friendly and superfast websites.

Next.js is a rising star of modern JavaScript. It is a powerful tool that can save a lot of time by doing all the under-the-hood processing required to bring a universal applications to life.

Who this book is for

This book is for skilled professionals seeking a comprehensive guide on how to build a flexible, scalable, and well-designed universal JavaScript application with server-side rendering capabilities using Next.js.

This book will also help developers discover what server-side rendering is and get to grips with what the bleeding edge of the technology has to offer in its current state.

We will guide users through the following challenges:

- Performance of single-page applications
- SEO
- Blazing-fast rendering of the initial page when a customers visit the website
- Maximum reuse of modules on client and server sides
- What server-side rendering is, how it helps, and how to do it right

What this book covers

`Chapter 1`, *Introduction to Server-Side Rendering and Next.js*, explains the basics of frontend development, problem definition, what frameworks are available, and what problems they solve, what server-side rendering is, and why it is needed. This chapter explains the benefits of Next.js.

`Chapter 2`, *Next.js Fundamentals,* explains the fundamental things about building JavaScript apps and React apps in particular. It guides the reader through installation and the development/build life cycle of the Next.js application. You'll learn how to create website pages and wire them together through the website navigation. After that, styling and rich content approaches are explained.

`Chapter 3`, *Next.js Configuration,* will go into Webpack and Babel. It is a small chapter but definitely one worth mentioning, because it is very useful for advanced cases.

`Chapter 4`, *Next.js Data Flow,* explains the purpose of all JS applications: talking to the backend. We show different approaches, including vanilla Next JS flow, with no frameworks, which is useful for understanding the essence of interaction before moving on to look at more advanced techniques.

`Chapter 5`, *Application Life Cycle Handlers and Business Logic,* demonstrates the most important and frequently asked questions about React-based application architecture and patterns. We explain how to design and implement the core modules, such as logging and authentication, and then move on to more complex solutions for access control and business rules management.

`Chapter 6`, *Continuous Integration,* explores how to prepare the app for automatic deployment and why unit and end-to-end tests are important prerequisites. You will learn how to write tests and use online continuous integration tools.

`Chapter 7`, *Containers,* provides information about virtual machine containers exploring, why they are useful. You will learn about the most popular container framework, Docker, and how to configure an image for it. After that, you'll learn how to deploy your application to online services that provide container-based infrastructure.

To get the most out of this book

Basic knowledge of JavaScript and Node.js, networking, software design patterns, and server-side and client-side programming is required. You will need a Git client, Node.js, and any text editor to be installed.

Download the example code files

You can download the example code files for this book from your account at `www.packtpub.com`. If you purchased this book elsewhere, you can visit `www.packtpub.com/support` and register to have the files emailed directly to you.

You can download the code files by following these steps:

1. Log in or register at `www.packtpub.com`.
2. Select the **SUPPORT** tab.
3. Click on **Code Downloads & Errata**.
4. Enter the name of the book in the **Search** box and follow the onscreen instructions.

Once the file is downloaded, please make sure that you unzip or extract the folder using the latest version of:

- WinRAR/7-Zip for Windows
- Zipeg/iZip/UnRarX for Mac
- 7-Zip/PeaZip for Linux

The code bundle for the book is also hosted on GitHub at `https://github.com/PacktPublishing/Next.js-Quick-Start-Guide`. In case there's an update to the code, it will be updated on the existing GitHub repository.

We also have other code bundles from our rich catalog of books and videos available at `https://github.com/PacktPublishing/`. Check them out!

Download the color images

We also provide a PDF file that has color images of the screenshots/diagrams used in this book. You can download it here: `http://www.packtpub.com/sites/default/files/downloads/NextDotjsQuickStartGuide_ColorImages.pdf`.

Conventions used

There are a number of text conventions used throughout this book.

`CodeInText`: Indicates code words in text, database table names, folder names, filenames, file extensions, pathnames, dummy URLs, user input, and Twitter handles. Here is an example: "Mount the downloaded `WebStorm-10*.dmg` disk image file as another disk in your system."

A block of code is set as follows:

```
import 'isomorphic-fetch';

        (async () => {
            const res = await fetch(...); // already polyfilled
        })();
```

When we wish to draw your attention to a particular part of a code block, the relevant lines or items are set in bold:

```
async getInitialProps({store}) {
  await store.dispatch({type: 'FOO', payload: 'foo'}); // this could be
async
  return {custom: 'custom'};
}
```

Any command-line input or output is written as follows:

```
$ npm install isomorphic-fetch --save
```

Bold: Indicates a new term, an important word, or words that you see onscreen. For example, words in menus or dialog boxes appear in the text like this. Here is an example: "Select **System info** from the **Administration** panel."

Warnings or important notes appear like this.

Tips and tricks appear like this.

Get in touch

Feedback from our readers is always welcome.

General feedback: Email `feedback@packtpub.com` and mention the book title in the subject of your message. If you have questions about any aspect of this book, please email us at `questions@packtpub.com`.

Errata: Although we have taken every care to ensure the accuracy of our content, mistakes do happen. If you have found a mistake in this book, we would be grateful if you would report this to us. Please visit `www.packtpub.com/submit-errata`, selecting your book, clicking on the Errata Submission Form link, and entering the details.

Piracy: If you come across any illegal copies of our works in any form on the Internet, we would be grateful if you would provide us with the location address or website name. Please contact us at `copyright@packtpub.com` with a link to the material.

If you are interested in becoming an author: If there is a topic that you have expertise in and you are interested in either writing or contributing to a book, please visit `authors.packtpub.com`.

Reviews

Please leave a review. Once you have read and used this book, why not leave a review on the site that you purchased it from? Potential readers can then see and use your unbiased opinion to make purchase decisions, we at Packt can understand what you think about our products, and our authors can see your feedback on their book. Thank you!

For more information about Packt, please visit `packtpub.com`.

1 Introduction to Server-Side Rendering and Next.js

For quite some time, client-server architecture was one of the most widespread patterns in large-scale software development. Even systems that run purely on one computer are often designed this way. This allows us to clearly separate concerns: the server takes care of heavy business logic, persistent storage, accessing data from third-party services, and so on, and the client is responsible solely for presentation to end users.

This architecture also allows us to have multiple clients connected to one backend: mobile apps, IoT devices, third-party REST API consumers (for example, external developers), and the web, for example.

In the early days of web development, it was not that way though. Servers were responsible for everything. Usually, it was a combination of DB, app itself, template engine, a bunch of static assets (images, CSS, and so on) all baked together into a monolithic app. Later on, it became obvious that this kind of architecture does not scale well.

Nowadays, the modern web is moving back to client-server architecture with a clean separation of concerns and concrete responsibilities for each component. Server-side apps deal with data and client-side apps deal with presentation of that data.

We will cover the following topics in this chapter:

- What is a single-page app?
- Introduction to React
- Single-page app performance issues
- Server-side rendering with React

What is a single-page app?

A single-page app implements this architecture for web clients: the JavaScript app launches from a web page and then runs entirely in the browser. All visual changes on the website happen as a reaction to user actions and the data received from the remote APIs.

It is called single-page because the server does not render pages for the client; it always delivers the same minimalistic markup required to bootstrap the JS app. All page rendering and navigation happens purely on the client, using JavaScript, which utilizes History APIs to dynamically swap page contents and URLs in the location bar.

The advantages that this approach gives are that the client can run something in the background between page transitions, and the client does not have to re-download and re-render the entire page in order to swap only the main content. Unfortunately, it also brings drawbacks, because now the client is responsible for all state changes. For the synchronization of such changes across the entire interface, it must know when to load the data and what particular data. In other words, a server-generated app is conceptually a way simpler thing, thanks to the REST service + JS client.

Creating JS Modules, code sharing, code splitting, and bundling

Separation of concerns is one of the key principles in software design, and since each entity in the code has to be isolated from others, it makes sense to put them into separate files to simplify the navigation and ensure isolation.

Modern JS applications consist of modules that can have exports and imports. JS modules export some entities and may consume exported entities from other modules.

In this book, we will use the latest JS syntax with classes, arrow functions, spread operators, and so on. If you are not familiar with this syntax, you can always refer to it here: `http://exploringjs.com`.

The simplest JS module looks like this:

```
// A.js:
export const noop = () => {};
```

This file now has a named export, `noop`, which is an arrow function that does nothing.

Now in `B.js`, we can import a function from the `A.js` file:

```
//B.js:
import {noop} from "./A.js";
noop();
```

In the real world, dependencies are much more complex and modules can export dozens of entities and import dozens of other modules, including those from NPM. The module system in JS allows us to statically trace all dependencies and figure out ways to optimize them.

If the client downloads all JS in a straightforward way (for example, initially downloading one JS file, parsing its dependencies, and recursively downloading them and their deps), then load time will be dramatic, first of all because network interaction takes time. Secondly, because parsing also takes time. Simultaneous connections are often limited by browser (the amount of HTTP threads) and HTTP 2.0, which allows us to transfer many files through one connection, is not yet available everywhere, so it makes sense to bundle all assets into one big bundle and deliver them all at once.

In order to do this, we can use a bundler like Webpack or Rollup. These bundlers are capable of tracing all dependencies starting from the initial module up to leaf ones and packing those modules together in a single bundle. Also, if configured, they allow us to minify the bundle using UglifyJS or any other compressor; this reduces the bundle size dramatically. Minification is a process where all unnecessary things are stripped out of the bundle, such as whitespaces and comments, all variables are named `a`, `b`, and so on, and all syntax constructions are simplified. After minification, we can also `gzip` the output if the server and client allow this.

But the bundle approach also have caveats. A bundle may contain things that are not required to render a particular requested page. Basically, the client can download a huge initial bundle but in fact need only 30-40% of it.

Modern bundlers allow us to split the app into smaller chunks and progressively load them on demand. In order to create a code split point, we can use the dynamic import syntax:

```
//B.js:
import('./A.js').then(({noop}) => {
 noop();
});
```

Now, the build tool can see that certain modules should not be included in the initial chunk and can be loaded on demand. But on the other hand, if those chunks are too granular, we will return to the starting point with tons of small files.

Unfortunately, if chunks are less granular, then most likely they will have some modules included in more than one chunk. Those common modules (primarily the ones installed from NPM) could be moved to so-called common chunks. The goal is to find an optimal balance between initial bundle size, common chunk size, and the size of code-split chunks. Webpack (or other bundlers such as Parcel or Rollup) can optimize it a bit, but a certain amount of manual tuning is required for best results.

Introduction to React

In this section, we will create a simple React-based project and will learn how this library works and what its core concepts are.

Let's create an empty project folder and initialize NPM:

```
$ mkdir learn-react
$ cd learn-react
$ npm init
$ npm install react react-dom --save
```

The quickest way to get started with React is to use the react-scripts package:

```
$ npm install react-scripts --save-dev
```

Now, let's add a start script to `package.json`:

```
{
  "scripts": {
    "start": "react-scripts start"
  }
}
```

NPM auto-binds CLI scripts installed in the `node_modules/.bin` directory along with the packages, so we can use them in `package.json` scripts directly.

The smallest possible setup for a React app is the following: we need a landing HTML page and one script with the app.

Let's start with the bedrock HTML:

```
<!--public/index.html-->
<!DOCTYPE html>
<html>
<head>
  <meta charset="utf-8">
  <title>Learn React</title>
</head>
<body>
  <div id="app"></div>
</body>
</html>
```

And here is the main JS file:

```
//src/index.js:
import React from "react";
import {render} from "react-dom";
render(
  <h1>It works!</h1>,
  document.getElementById('app')
);
```

This is it. Now, we can run the command to start the development server:

```
$ npm start
```

It will open port `3000` on the `localhost`. Open the URL `http://localhost:3000` in your browser; the `index.js` script will be run and the render function will render an HTML page with "It works!" in it.

To learn more about React JSX, I encourage you to take a look at the official documentation: `https://reactjs.org/docs/introducing-jsx.html`. This chapter will only briefly cover the main aspects that are essential for Next.js apps.

The simplest React component is just a function that takes props as an argument and returns JSX:

```
const Cmp = ({children, ...props}) => (<div {...props}>{children}</div>);
```

JSX is HTML with the ability to insert and execute JS in it. In this example, we inject variables into a tag as properties and as content.

A more complicated component may have state:

```
class Cmp extends React.Component {
  state = {value: 'init'};
  onClick = (event) => { this.setState({value: 'clicked'}); };
  render() {
    return (
      <button onClick={this.onClick}>{this.state.value}</button>
    );
  }
}
```

Components may have static properties:

```
class Cmp extends React.Component {
  static foo = 'foo';
}
```

or

```
Cmp.foo = 'foo';
```

These static properties are often used to describe some meta-information about the components:

```
import PropTypes from "prop-types";
Cmp.propTypes = {
  propName: PropTypes.string
};
```

Next.js utilizes static properties heavily and we will show you how later.

The simplest way to achieve code splitting in a React application is to store the entire progressively-loaded component in the state:

```
class Cmp extends React.Component {
  state = {Sub: null};
  onClick = async (event) => {
    const Sub = (await import('./path/to/Sub.js')).default;
    this.setState({Sub});
  };
  render() {
    const {Sub} = this.state;
    return (
      <div>
        <button onClick={this.onClick}>Load</button>
        <Sub/>
      </div>
```

```
      );
    }
  }
```

Do not use this straightforward way with Next.js, as it will not work in Server-Side Rendering mode. In the next chapter, we will show you how to do it properly.

Another way to achieve code splitting is to use the React Router.

All React components have life cycle hooks that can be utilized, for example, to load the data from a remote server:

```
class Cmp extends React.Component {
  state = {data: null};
  async componentWillMount() {
    const data = await (await fetch('https://example.com')).json();
    this.setState({data});
  }
  render() {
    const {data} = this.state;
    return (
      <pre>
        {JSON.stringify(data)}
      </pre>
    );
  }
}
```

The React API is of course much bigger than what was covered here, so please refer to the official documentation for more info. The things mentioned here are absolutely essential for Next.js, which is why we mentioned them.

Why single-page apps suffer performance issues

In order to start, **single-page apps** (**SPA**) have to download lots of assets to the client: JS files with the app itself, CSS files with styles, images, media, and so on. It is impossible to develop a large-scale JS app without any kind of modularization, so most JS apps consist of numerous small JS files (the modules mentioned before). CSS files are also usually separated by some criteria: per component, per page, and so on.

The nature of SPAs forces them to have heavy API traffic. Basically, any user action that has to be persisted requires an API call. Pulling data from persistent storage also requires API calls. By persistent storage, here I mean the database or any other similar service that can be accessed from many different devices/browsers and will store this data for long periods of time.

Both of these aspects bring us to the most terrible SPA performance issue: large initial load time. There have been studies that clearly show the correlation between the load time and page views, conversion, and other vital metrics. On average, customers leave the page if it fails to load within 2-3 seconds.

Another big issue is **search engine optimization** (**SEO**). Search engines tend to give higher ranks to pages that load quicker. Plus, only recently have crawlers learned how to parse and crawl SPAs properly.

How do we deal with this?

Assume we have found a good balance between initial chunk and on-demand chunks. We have applied compression and good cache strategies, but still there is an API layer that also has to be optimized for initial load.

Potentially, we can combine all API requests in one huge request and load it. But different pages need different data, so we can't create a request that will fit all. Also, some of the data requires client-side processing before we can make a subsequent request for more data. Modern API techniques such as GraphQL allow us to solve the problem in one way, and we will talk about this later in the book, but this still does not address the issue with not-so-smart search engine crawlers.

Sad? Yes. There is a solution for that though. It is called server-side rendering.

Server side rendering

Back in the old days, web pages were served as is by static servers. All navigation and interaction were based on those pages; you had to transition from one page to another, nothing was dynamic, and you could not show or hide a block of text, or do something similar.

Later, servers started to use templates to deliver HTML to the client. Languages such as Java, PHP, Python, ASP, VBScript, Perl, and Ruby were suitable for such tasks. Those pages were called server-generated. The interaction though was still the same: page transitions.

Then JavaScript and VBScript came into play for very simple client-side user interaction, just some hover effects and simple scripts here and there to show or hide server-generated content. Some time later, more complicated scenarios were introduced and the bias shifted towards the client side. Servers started to generate not only full templates, but also replaceable fragments to reflect more in-place changes, such as when the client sends a form via AJAX and receives from the server the HTML of this form with validation errors, client only swapped HTML pieces, it was not responsible for templating.

Later on, due to the shift towards REST APIs, a cleaner separation of concerns brought the industry away from server-generated approaches to fully JS-driven apps, which were capable of rendering the pure data into HTML by using client-side templates.

But in order to more efficiently load the initial data for a JS app, we can utilize the server-generated approach a little bit. We can render the initial markup on the server and then let the JS app take it over later. The main assumption here is the fact that the server-side renderer is usually much closer to the API server, ideally in the same data center, and thus it has much better connection and way more bandwidth than remote clients (browsers in our case). It also can utilize all benefits of HTTP2 or any other protocol to maintain fast data exchange.

The server can optimize rendering time by caching the results from rendering individual components or entire pages, indexed on a serialization of the parameters that affect the output - that are used by the component. This is particularly true of components or entire pages that will be viewed repeatedly in the same state, either just by one user or potentially by many different users. Where appropriate, this strategy may even allow the server-side renderer to reduce load on the API server, if cached component renders are given a TTL.

The server-side renderer is capable of doing all those chained requests much faster than clients, and all the codebase can be pre-loaded and pre-parsed. It can also use more aggressive data caching strategies, since invalidation can also be centrally maintained.

To decrease code duplication, we would like to use the same technology and the same templates both on the client and on the server. Such an app is called universal or isomorphic.

The general approach is as follows: we take the Node.js server, install a web framework, and start listening to incoming requests. On every request that matches a certain URL, we take the client scripts and use them to bootstrap the initial state of the app for the given page. Then, we serialize the resulting HTML and data, bake it together, and send it to the client.

The client immediately shows the markup and then bootstraps the app on the client, applying initial data and state, and hence taking control.

The next page transition will happen completely on the client; it will load data from regular API endpoints just like before. One of the trickiest parts of this approach is to make sure that the same page with the same HTML will be rendered both on the client and on the server, which means we need to make sure the client app will be bootstrapped in a certain state that will result in the same HTML.

This brings us to the choice of framework. Not all client-side frameworks are capable of server-side rendering; for instance, it would be quite challenging to write a jQuery app that will pick up state and render itself correctly on top of existing HTML.

How to do server-side rendering with React

Luckily, React is built with two main concepts in mind: it's state driven and it is capable of rendering to plain HTML. React is often used with React Router, so let's take this and explain how to render your React app on a server.

React-based server-side rendering frameworks, why Next.js

Nowadays, there are few competitors in the React-based server-side rendering market. We can divide them into the following categories:

- Drop-in dynamic solutions (Next.js, Electrode, After)
- Drop-in static solutions (Gatsby, React Static)
- Custom solutions

The main difference between first two approaches is the way the app is built and served.

A static solution makes a static HTML build (with all possible router pages), and then this build can be served by a static server such as Nginx, Apache, or any other. All HTML is pre-baked, as well as the initial state. This is very suitable for websites with incremental content updates that happen infrequently, for example, for a blog.

The dynamic solution generates HTML on the fly every time the client requests it. This means we can put in any dynamic logic, or any dynamic HTML blocks such as per-request ads and so on. But the drawback is that it requires a long-running server.
This server has to be monitored and ideally should become a cluster of servers for redundancy to make sure it's highly available.

We will make the main focus of this book dynamic solutions, as they are more flexible and more complex but also require deeper understanding.

Lets dive deeper into a custom solution using only React and React Router.

Let's install the router and special package to configure routes statically (it's impossible to generate purely dynamic routes on a server):

```
npm i --save react-router-dom react-router-config
```

Now, let's configure the routes:

```
// routes.js
const routes = [
  {
    path: '/',
    exact: true,
    component: Index
  },
  {
    path: '/list',
    component: List
  }
];
export default routes;
```

The main app entry point should look like this:

```
// index.js
import React from 'react';
import {render} from 'react-dom';
import BrowserRouter from 'react-router-dom/BrowserRouter';
import {renderRoutes} from 'react-router-config';
import routes from './routes';

const Router = () => {
  return (
    <BrowserRouter>
      {renderRoutes(routes)}
    </BrowserRouter>
  )
```

```
};

render(<Router />, document.getElementById('app'));
```

On the server, we will have the following:

```
import express from 'express';
import React from 'react';
import { renderToString } from 'react-dom/server';
import StaticRouter from 'react-router-dom/StaticRouter';
import { renderRoutes } from 'react-router-config';
import routes from './src/routes';

const app = express();

app.get('*', (req, res) => {
  let context = {}; // pre-fill somehow
  const content = renderToString(
    <StaticRouter location={req.url} context={context}>
      {renderRoutes(routes)}
    </StaticRouter>
  );
  res.render('index', {title: 'SSR', content });
});
```

But, this will simply render the page with no data. In order to prepopulate data into the page, we need to do the following, both in the component and in the server:

1. Each data-enabled component must expose a method that the server should call during route resolution
2. The server iterates over all matched components and utilizes exposed methods
3. The server collects the data and puts it into storage
4. The server renders the HTML using routes and data from storage
5. The server sends to the client the resulting HTML, along with data
6. The client initializes using the HTML and prepopulates the state using data

We intentionally won't show steps 3 and onward, because there is no generic way for pure React and React Router. For storage, most solutions will use Redux and this is a whole another topic. So, here we just show the basic principle:

```
// list.js
import React from "react";

const getText = async () => (await (await
fetch('https://api.github.com/users/octocat')).text());
```

```
export default class List extends React.Component {

  state = {text: ''};

  static async getInitialProps(context) {
    context.text = await getText();
  }

  async componentWillMount() {
    const text = await getText();
    this.setState({text})
  }
  render() {
    const {staticContext} = this.props;
    let {text} = this.state;
    if (staticContext && !text) text = staticContext.text;
    return (
      <pre>Text: {text}</pre>
    );
  }

}

// server.js
// all from above
app.get('*', (req, res) => {
  const {url} = req;
  const matches = matchRoutes(routes, url);
  const context = {};
  const promises = matches.map(({route}) => {
    const getInitialProps = route.component.getInitialProps;
    return getInitialProps ? getInitialProps(context) :
Promise.resolve(null)
  });
  return Promise.all(promises).then(() => {
    console.log('Context', context);
    const content = renderToString(
      <StaticRouter location={url} context={context}>
        {renderRoutes(routes)}
      </StaticRouter>
    );
    res.render('index', {title: 'SSR', content});
  });
});
```

The reason why we are not covering those aspects is because even after heavy development, it becomes obvious that the custom solution still has quirks and glitches, primarily because React Router was not meant to be used on a server, so every custom solution always has some hacks. Even the authors of React Router say that they decided not to use server-side rendering in their projects. So, it would be much better to take a stable/standard solution that was built with server-side rendering in mind from day one.

Among other competitors, Next.js stands out as one of the pioneers of this approach; this framework is currently the most popular. It offers a very convenient API, easy installation, zero configuration, and a huge community. Electrode may be more flexible and powerful than Next.js, but it has extremely complicated configuration. After this is a Next.js-alike framework, which is built on top of React Router, Helmet and other familiar libraries, but the community is still relatively small so far, although it definitely worth to mention.

A full comparison is available in my article here: `https://medium.com/disdj/solutions-for-react-app-development-f9fcaeba504`.

Summary

In this chapter, we learned how web apps evolved over time from simple server-generated pages to single-page apps, and then back to server-generated pages with SPAs on top. We learned what React JS is and how to do server-rendering of a React application.

In the next chapter, we will use this knowledge to build a more advanced application that still follows these core principles.

2
Next.js fundamentals

In this chapter, we will learn the very basics of Next.js, such as installation, development, and production usage; how to create simple pages and add components to them; and how to apply styles and add media therefore be covered:

- Installation
- Developer mode
- Pages
- Production mode
- Routing
- Dynamic routing
- SEO-friendly routing
- Styles
- Media
- Graphs

Installation of Next.js

First, create an empty project folder and initialize npm in it:

```
$ mkdir next-js-condensed
$ cd next-js-condensed
$ npm init
```

After that, let's install the Next.js package:

```
$ npm install nextjs@latest --save-dev
$ npm install react@latest react-dom@latest --save
```

We save Next.js to `devDependencies` to clearly separate dependencies for the client and for the server. Server-side dependencies will be in the `devDependencies` section; the client's will be in the regular section.

If you're using Git or any similar source control tool, it makes sense to add an ignore file that will remove the build artifacts folder from source control. We show an example `.gitignore` file here:

```
.DS_Store
.idea
.next
.vscode
build
coverage
node_modules
npm-debug*
out
yarn-debug*
yarn-error*
```

Running Next.js in developer mode

In order to start the server, by convention we need to define a start script in `package.json`, so we will add the following there:

```
{
  "scripts": {
    "start": "next"
  }
}
```

Now, you can start the server by typing this in the console:

```
$ npm start
```

Now, if you visit `http://localhost:3000` in your browser, you will see the running server.

Creating your first Next.js page

Now, let's create the first page and place it in the `pages` folder:

```
// pages/index.js
import React from "react";
export default () => (<div>Hello, World!</div>);
```

Now, if you run the dev server (`npm start`) and visit `http://localhost:3000`, you will see this page:

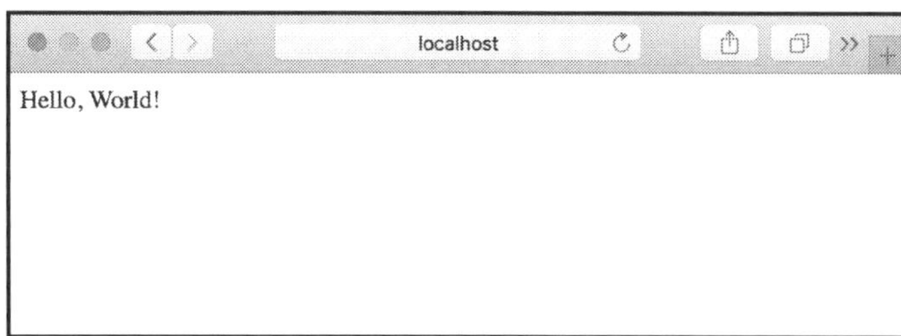

Now, let's see how Next.js handles errors in your files:

```
// pages/index.js
import React from "react";
export default () => (<div><p>Hello, World!</div>);
//                              ^ here we purposely not closing this tag
```

Then, reload the page to see this:

localhost

Error in ./pages/index.js

Module build failed: SyntaxError: Unterminated JSX contents (6:10)

```
  4 |     <div>
  5 |         <p>Hello, World!
> 6 |     </div>
    |          ^
  7 | );
```

Running a Next.js production build

Next.js supports two kinds of production usage, static and dynamic, the main difference being that a static build can be served by any static HTTP server as a static website, whereas dynamic usage means that there will be a Next.js server that executes the production build:

1. Static mode is best suited for simple websites with no dynamic content. We need to add a script to `package.json`:

```
{
  "scripts": {
   "build": "next build",
   "static": "next export"
 }
}
```

2. Then, we have to add a `next.config.js` with a path map (this was fixed in `6.0.0`; you no longer have to do it for 1-1 matches of filesystems and URLs):

```
// next.config.js
module.exports = {
    exportPathMap: () => ({
        '/': {page: '/'}
    })
};
```

3. Now, we run this:

```
$ npm run build
$ npm run static
```

   This will create a static build that we can deploy somewhere. We will cover this in later chapters.

4. In order to build and run the site for dynamic production mode, we will add more scripts to `package.json`:

```
{
  "scripts": {
    "build": "next build",
    "server": "next start"
  }
}
```

5. Then, in the console, run this:

```
$ npm run build
$ npm run server
```

This will make the build and run the production server using that `build`.

Making Next.js routing

Now that we know how to make Next.js routing, let's make another page:

```
// pages/second.js
import React from "react";
export default () => (<div>Second</div>);
```

This new page is accessible via `http://localhost:3000/second`.

Now, let's add a link to that second page to the index page.

If we use a simple `<a>` tag for this, it will work, of course, but it will perform a regular server request instead of client-side navigation, so performance will be much worse: the client will reload all the initialization payloads, and will be forced to re-initialize the entire app.

1. In order to do proper client-side navigation, we need to import a link component from Next.js:

```
// pages/index.js
import React from "react";
import Link from "next/link";
export default () => (<div><Link href="/second"><a>Second</a>
</Link></div>);
```

2. Here, we added a new link to the page content; notice that we have added an empty `<a>` tag:

```
<Link href="/second"><a>Second</a></Link>
```

`<Link>` is a wrapper on top of any component that can accept the `onClick` prop; we will talk about that a bit later.

3. Now, open `http://localhost:3000`, click the link, and verify that page is not reloading by looking in the network tab of the developer tools.
4. So, what if we'd like to apply styles to the link? We should apply them not on `<Link>` but on the `<a>` component – separation of concerns at its finest.

`<Link>` accepts all nav-related props, whereas `<a>` (or any other component) is used for presentation (styles, look, and feel).

```
<Link href="/second"><button style={{fontWeight:
'bold'}}>Second</button></Link>
```

This code still works as expected. Please keep in mind that this is not an SEO-friendly way to create a link; we use `<button>` to illustrate that any clickable component can be used. You should use `<a>` instead of `<button>` for SEO.

Link is also capable of one interesting thing: by default it uses lazy loading of the underlying nav page, but for maximum performance you may use `<Link prefetch>`, which will allow instant transition.

Now, let's code a more complicated case for a custom button-like component:

1. In order to pass a `href` prop to the underlying component (in case the top-level component will not be recognized as a link/button), we need to add a `passHref` prop.
2. We also can import with Router **HOC** (**Higher Order Component**) from next/router to allow resolution of URLs in order to highlight if the desired route is already selected:

```
// components/Btn.js
import React from 'react';
import {withRouter} from 'next/router';

const Btn = ({href, onClick, children, router}) => ( // router
prop is injected by withRouter HOC
    <span>
        <button onClick={onClick} style={{fontWeight :
```

```
            router.pathname === href ? 'bold' : ''}}>
                {children}
            </button>
        </span>
);

export default withRouter(Btn);
```

HOC is a function that takes a component and wraps it with some extra functionality. Usually, HOCs provide extra props to children components; in the case of Router, a wrapped component will receive `router` and other props.

3. Now, let's create a top `nav` component for all pages:

```
// components/Nav.js
import React from "react";
import Link from 'next/link';
import Btn from "./Btn";

export default () => (
    <div>
        <Link href="/" passHref><Btn>Index</Btn></Link>
        <Link href="/second" passHref><Btn>Second</Btn></Link>
    </div>
);
```

4. And now, let's use it in pages:

```
// pages/index.js
import React from 'react';
import Nav from "../components/Nav";

export default () => (
    <div>
        <Nav/>
        <hr/>
        Index
    </div>
);

// pages/second.js
import React from 'react';
import Nav from "../components/Nav";

export default () => (
    <div>
        <Nav/>
        <hr/>
```

```
            Second
        </div>
    );
```

Dynamic routing

Of course, no real app can live with only static URLs based on just pages, so let's add a bit of dynamic routing to our app:

1. Let's start with a small data source stub:

```
// data/posts.js
export default [
    {title: 'Foo'},
    {title: 'Bar'},
    {title: 'Baz'},
    {title: 'Qux'}
];
```

2. Now, let's connect it to our index page:

```
// pages/index.js
import React from 'react';
import Link from "next/link";
import Nav from "../components/Nav";
import posts from "../data/posts";

export default () => (
    <div>

        <Nav/>

        <hr/>

        <ul>
      {posts.map((post, index) => (
          <li key={index}>
              <Link href={{pathname: '/second', query: {id: index}}}>
                  <a>{post.title}</a>
              </Link>
          </li>
      ))}
  </ul>

</div>
);
```

Here, we imported the data source and iterated over it to produce some simple `nav` links, as you can see; for convenience, we may also use `href` as a URL object. Next.js will serialize it into a standard string.

3. Now, let's update the second page:

```
// pages/second.js
import React from 'react';
import Nav from "../components/Nav";
import posts from "../data/posts";

export default ({url: {query: {id}}}) => (
    <div>
        <Nav/>
        <hr/>
        <h1>{posts[id].title}</h1>
    </div>
);
```

Now, if we visit `http://localhost:3000`, we will see a clickable list of posts, each of them leading to a dedicated dynamic page.

Unfortunately, if we now visit the second page directly from our `Nav` component (by clicking the top menu button) we will get a nasty error. We purposely put in a link to a nonexistent page for simplicity, but let's assume somebody did that by mistake. Let's make the error look prettier at least. We should import a special Next.js Error component and return it in case of any errors:

```
// pages/second.js
import React from 'react';
import Error from 'next/error';
import Nav from "../components/Nav";
import posts from "../data/posts";

export default ({url: {query: {id}}}) => (
    (posts[id]) ? (
        <div>
            <Nav/>
            <hr/>
            <h1>{posts[id].title}</h1>
        </div>
    ) : (
        <Error statusCode={404}/>
    )
);
```

4. We have added an import:

```
import Error from 'next/error';
```

5. And, we wrapped the component in a ternary operator:

```
export default ({url: {query: {id}}}) => (
    (posts[id]) ? (...) : (<Error statusCode={404}/>)
);
```

6. This will return a nice Next.js 404 Page Not Found error page.

If we now visit the "Second" link from the top menu we will hit 404. That's by design to show how 404 works. There will be no ID and hence no post loaded, so ternary condition will produce `Error` component.

Making Next.js routing masks – SEO-friendly URLs

If you look at the location bar of the browser when you visit the second page, you'll see something like `http://localhost:3000/second?id=0`, which is fine, but not pretty enough. We can add some niceness to the URL schema that we use. This is optional, but it's always good to have SEO-friendly URLs instead of query-string parameters.

In order to do that, we should use a special as `prop` of the `Link` component:

```
<Link as={`/post/${index}`} href={{pathname: '/second', query: {id:
index}}}>
    <a>{post.title}</a>
</Link>
```

But, if you visit such a link and reload the page, you will see 404 Page Not Found error. Why is that? It's because URL masking (a technology we just used) works on the client side at runtime, and when we reload the page we need to teach the server to work with such URLs.

In order to do that, we will have to make a custom server. Luckily, Next.js offers useful tools to simplify this.

Let's start with installing Express:

```
$ npm install --save-dev express
```

The server code should look like this:

```
// /server.js
const express = require('express');
const next = require('next');

const port = 3000;
// use default NodeJS environment variable to figure out dev mode
const dev = process.env.NODE_ENV !== 'production';
const app = next({dev});
const handle = app.getRequestHandler();
const server = express();

server.get('/post/:id', (req, res) => {
    const actualPage = '/second';
    const queryParams = {id: req.params.id};
    app.render(req, res, actualPage, queryParams);
});

server.get('*', (req, res) => { // pass through everything to NextJS
    return handle(req, res)
});

app.prepare().then(() => {

    server.listen(port, (err) => {
        if (err) throw err
        console.log('NextJS is ready on http://localhost:' + port);
    });

}).catch(e => {

    console.error(e.stack);
    process.exit(1);

});
```

The main thing in this code is the following code block:

```
server.get('/post/:id', (req, res) => {
    const actualPage = '/second';
    const queryParams = {id: req.params.id};
    app.render(req, res, actualPage, queryParams);
});
```

It uses a URL parser to figure out the URL param and provide it to the actual page as a query string param, which is understandable by the Next.js server-side renderer.

In order to launch this as usual, we need to alter the `package.json` scripts section:

```
{
  "scripts": {
    "start": "node server.js"
  }
}
```

Now, we run this as we did before:

```
$ npm start
```

Then, we directly open a post, `http://localhost:3000/post/0` and, it will work as expected.

Keep in mind that visiting Second link from top menu will produce 404. That's by design as explained before.

Dynamic Component Loading (aka Lazy Components)

Even though Next.js can split your app into route-based asynchronously loaded chunks, it is always a good idea to split further if it is needed. The less unnecessary code the user loads up front, the better.

The technique is very simple and completely supported by Next.js:

```
import dynamic from 'next/dynamic';
```

And then, anywhere on demand, we can do the loading:

```
import dynamic from 'next/dynamic'

const FooDynamic = dynamic(import('../components/Foo'))

export default class Page extends React.Component {
  state = {show: false};
  show = () => this.setState({show: true});
  render() {
```

```
      return (
        this.state.show ? <FooDynamic/> : <button
onClick={this.show}>Show!</button>
      );
    }

  }
```

Here, the component will not be loaded until it is actually placed on the page (that is, rendered).

We can even define the dynamic component with a loader:

```
const loading = () => <div>Loading</div>;
const FooDynamicLoader = dynamic(
  import('../components/Foo'),
  {loading}
);
```

Also, we can load multiple components at once:

```
const Bundle = dynamic({
  // you can add or remove components based on props
  modules: props => ({
    Foo: import('../components/Foo'),
    Bar: import('../components/Bar')
  }),
  render: (props, {Foo, Bar}) => (
    <div>
      <h1>
        {props.title}
      </h1>
      <Foo />
      <Bar />
    </div>
  )
});

export default () => (
  <Bundle title="Dynamic Bundle" />);
```

Adding styles to an application – CSS in JS

There are many ways a Next.js app can be styled.

The simplest way is to use inline styles. Obviously, this is the worst possible way, but we'll start small:

```
const selectedStyles = {
    fontWeight: 'bold'
};

const regularStyles = {
    fontWeight: 'normal'
};

const Btn = ({href, onClick, children, pathname}) => (
    <button style={pathname === href ? selectedStyles : regularStyles}}>
        {children}
    </button>
);
```

Obviously, this does not scale at all. Luckily, Next.js offers a technique called JSS (one of many ways to have CSS in JS), and JSS can be used straight inside JSX to define styles:

```
// components/button.js
import React from 'react';
import {withRouter} from 'next/router';

export default withRouter(({href, onClick, children, router}) => (
    <span>
        <button onClick={onClick}
                className={router.pathname === href ? 'current' : ''}>
            {children}
        </button>
        <style jsx>{`
          button {
            color: blue;
            border: 1px solid;
            cursor: pointer;
          }

          button:hover {
            color: red;
          }

          button.current {
            font-weight: bold;
```

```
            }
        `}</style>
    </span>
));
```

This will create a scoped style sheet. If you want a global one, you should use `<style jsx global>`.

There is another new technique for Next.js 5+, which allows us to extend configuration with Webpack loader plugins. Fine-tuned configuration will be covered in the next chapter, so here we will briefly show the simple CSS example:

First, we need to install the plugin:

```
npm i @zeit/next-css --save-dev
```

Then, we should create a `next.config.js` file and add the following in there:

```
// /next.config.js
const withCss = require('@zeit/next-css');
module.exports = withCss({});
```

In order to properly place styles on a page, we should add a custom document (this will be explained in further detail in the next chapter):

```
// /pages/_document.js
import Document, {Head, Main, NextScript} from 'next/document';

export default class MyDocument extends Document {
    render() {
        return (
            <html>
            <Head>
                <link rel="stylesheet" href="/_next/static/style.css"/>
                <title>NextJS Condensed</title>
            </Head>
            <body>
            <Main/>
            <NextScript/>
            </body>
            </html>
        )
    }
}
```

Now, we can import CSS files just like any other import in JS:

```
// /pages/nav.js
import React from "react";
import Btn from "./Btn";
import Link from 'next/link';
import './Nav.css'; // the styles import

export default () => (
    <nav>
        <Link href="/" passHref><Btn>Index</Btn></Link>
        <Link href="/second" passHref><Btn>Second</Btn></Link>
    </nav>
);
```

The style sheet itself is a regular CSS file:

```
nav {
    background: #f6f6f6;
}
```

Now, when we reload the server, we will see the following on the page:

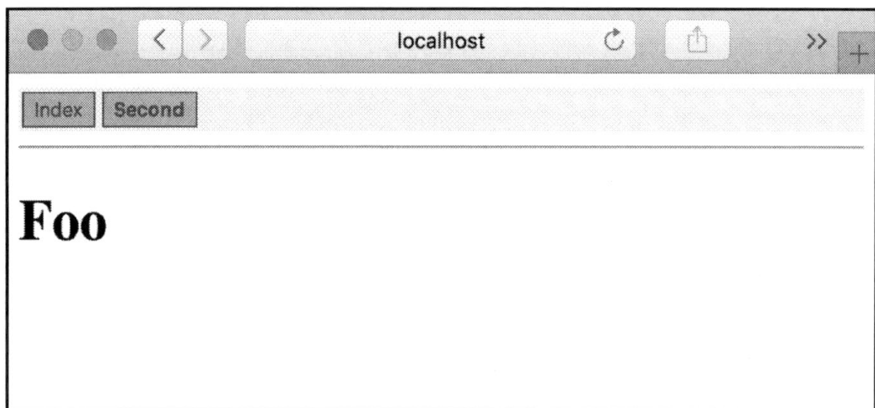

As you see, the buttons are blue on a gray background. It looks ugly, but this is just for demonstration.

Adding media content – images, video, and audio

Generally speaking, it's better to refer to images from CSS so that the entire presentation layer is configured in one place. It's usually a red flag when you want to insert an image in a JS component. We're not talking about image URLs coming from API responses; those are always inserted dynamically.

In this case, you should just refer to an image as you normally do. Next.js and Webpack will take care of this, and if the image is small enough, will even Base64-encode it and put it inline in CSS.

As a quick reference, let's add an icon to a `Nav` component:

```
// components/Nav.css
.logo-css {
    background: url(/static/js.jpg) no-repeat center center;
    background-size: cover;
}
.logo {
    background: url(/static/js.jpg) no-repeat center center;
    background-size: cover;
}
```

We must place the image in the `static` folder, otherwise it will not work via regular CSS.

Now, let's add a `span` to the `Nav` component:

```
// components/Nav.js
export default () => (
    <nav>
        <span className="logo logo-css"/>
    </nav>
);
```

Here is how it will look in the browser:

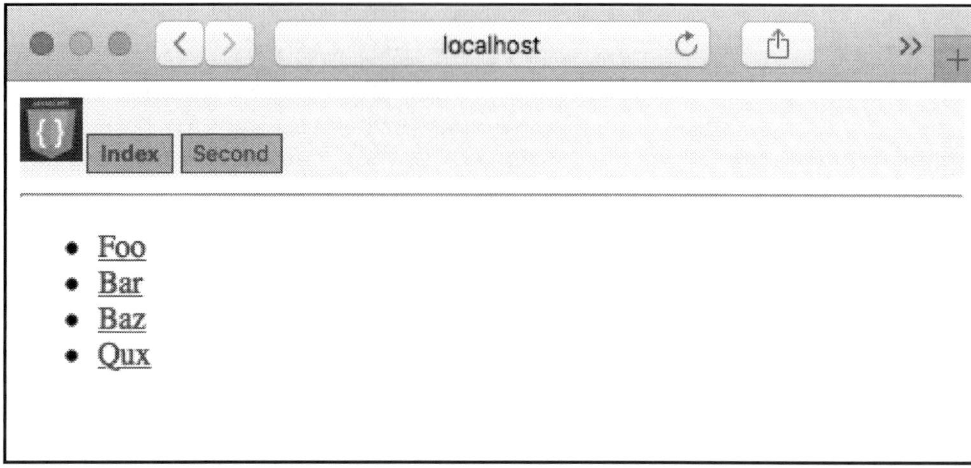

But, for those rare cases when we have to insert an image or any other media, Next.js provides a very easy and convenient way, as well via the static folder. Just add an image as you normally do in your HTML:

```
// components/Nav.js
export default () => (
    <nav>
        <span className="logo logo-css"/>
        <img src='/static/js.png' className="logo" alt="Logo"/>
    </nav>
);
```

But, with Next.js 5, there is a more modern way to do this.

We have to first install the plugin:

```
$ npm install --save-dev next-images
```

Next, add the usage of the plugin to `next.config.js`:

```
const withCss = require('@zeit/next-css');
const withImages = require('next-images');
module.exports = withImages(withCss({}));
```

And now, we can import an image like we import JS files. In this case, instead of real importing, only the pre-built URL will be imported:

```
// components/Nav.js
// ... previous imports
import PNG from '../static/js.png';

export default () => (
    <nav>
        <span className="logo logo-css"/>
        <img src='/static/js.png' className="logo" alt="Logo"/>
        <img src={PNG} className="logo" alt="Logo"/>
    </nav>
);
```

We can import any other media type exactly the same way, but for videos the static way is preferred.

Adding interactive graphs and charts

There are many graph/chart libraries available on the market, but for the sake of an example, we will use the one that is truly React-based and can deliver high performance.

1. The first step, as usual, is installation:

   ```
   $ npm i react-vis --save
   ```

2. Next, let's create a simple graph on the index page.

   We need to add library styles (this assumes that you have added the with Css plugin in the previous step):

   ```
   import "react-vis/dist/style.css";
   ```

3. Next, let's implement a simple graph; we should import the required parts:

```
    import {HorizontalGridLines, LineSeries, XAxis, XYPlot, YAxis} from
'react-vis';
```

4. Then, we can add a graph implementation, so the resulting page will look like this:

```
// pages/index.js
... other imports
import {HorizontalGridLines, LineSeries, XAxis, XYPlot, YAxis} from
'react-vis';
import "react-vis/dist/style.css";

export default () => (
    <div>

        ... other stuff that we had here

        <XYPlot
            width={300}
            height={300}>
            <HorizontalGridLines/>
            <LineSeries
                data={[
                    {x: 1, y: 10},
                    {x: 2, y: 5},
                    {x: 3, y: 15}
                ]}/>
            <XAxis/>
            <YAxis/>
        </XYPlot>

    </div>
);
```

This results in a nice graph in the browser:

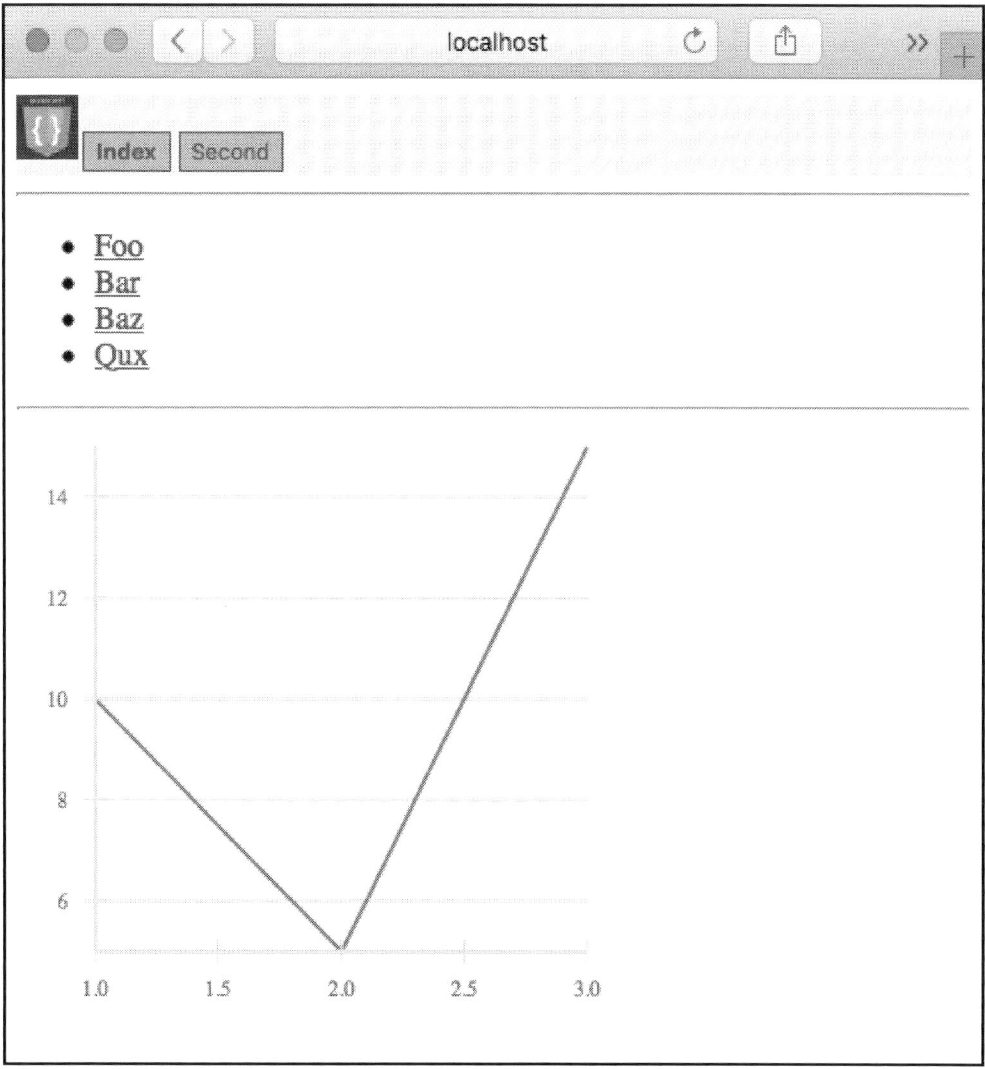

This graph is an SVG controlled by React and no other libraries, such as jQuery, are used.

Summary

In this chapter, we learned how to create pages, add components to them, make styles, and insert different kinds of media. In the next chapters, we will address more advanced topics, such as configuration.

3
Next.js Configuration

We have already touched on this topic slightly in the previous chapter, but this time let's dive a bit deeper into it.

Although Next.js provides lots and lots of perks out of the box, sometimes it is required to add some extra stuff, just like before, for CSS and image support.

Next.js, especially the latest version, offers a good amount of tools to customize the build and add lots of uncommon things.

In this chapter, we will learn about:

- Special pages
- How to make custom configurations
- How to customize Webpack; for example, how to add TypeScript support
- How to configure Babel

Special pages

Next.js allows us to affect the way a website will be rendered by placing special handlers for certain items.

The first one is `pages/_document.js`, which allows us to define the surroundings of the page, such as the *Head* section. This could be useful to change the page title, add meta information or styles, and so on.

Here is a minimal example:

```
// pages/_document.js
import Document, {Head, Main, NextScript} from 'next/document';

export default class MyDocument extends Document {
    render() {
```

```
            return (
                <html>
                <Head>
                    <title>NextJS Condensed</title>
                </Head>
                <body>
                <Main/>
                <NextScript/>
                </body>
                </html>
            )
        }
    }
```

In this example, we've configured the very basic surroundings of the actual markup that will be injected in the page straight in the `body` tag; also, we've added a `title` to the custom `Head` component.

The next special handler is `pages/_app.js`, which allows us to wrap ALL pages (including the error) in a special wrapper. You can use it to create layout or do things on the site level, for example to persist layout, store some state between page changes (such as logged in user information, or some global menu state, or anything that has to be displayed in more than one page), or perform `componentDidCatch` (this will be explained later). Here is an example:

```
// pages/_app.js
import App, {Container} from 'next/app';
import React from 'react';

export default class MyApp extends App {

  static async getInitialProps ({ Component, router, ctx }) {
    let pageProps = {};
    if (Component.getInitialProps) pageProps = await
Component.getInitialProps(ctx);
    return {pageProps};
  }

  state = {foo: ''};

  setFoo = (foo) => this.setState({foo});

  render () {
    const {Component, pageProps} = this.props
    return (<Container>
      <Component {...pageProps} foo={this.state.foo} setFoo={this.setFoo}/>
    </Container>);
```

```
    }

  }
```

The next one is the default 404 or 500 error handler, `pages/_error.js` (we will talk more about it in the following chapters; for now, let's just make a note that it exists):

```
// pages/_error.js
import React from 'react'

export default class Error extends React.Component {
  static getInitialProps({ res, err }) {
    const statusCode = res ? res.statusCode : err ? err.statusCode : null;
    return { statusCode }
  }

  render() {
    return (
      <p>
        {this.props.statusCode
          ? `An error ${this.props.statusCode} occurred on server`
          : 'An error occurred on client'}
      </p>
    )
  }
}
```

How to make custom configurations

In a nutshell, all Next.js configurations are done via `next.config.js`. With Next.js 5, this became even easier.

Let's create an empty project for experiments:

```
$ npm init
$ npm install react react-dom
```

Let's add `SASS` support as an example:

```
$ npm install next node-sass @zeit/next-sass --save-dev
```

Enhance the `scripts` section of `package.json`:

```
// package.json
{
    "scripts": {
        "start": "next"
    }
}
```

Next, we again have to create a custom document (the same as before):

```
// pages/_document.js
import Document, {Head, Main, NextScript} from 'next/document';

export default class MyDocument extends Document {
    render() {
        return (
            <html>
            <Head>
                <title>NextJS Condensed</title>
                <link rel="stylesheet" href="/_next/static/style.css"/>
            </Head>
            <body>
            <Main/>
            <NextScript/>
            </body>
            </html>
        )
    }
}
```

We're using the Next.js proprietary URL prefix for static files, `/_next/static/`, which is a default functionality.

Now, let's create a stylesheet using `SASS`:

```
// pages/index.sass
body
  font-family: Arial, sans-serif
  font-size: 12px
```

And, let's create an index page:

```
// pages/index.js
import React from 'react';
import "./index.sass";

export default () => (
    <div>
        Styled text
    </div>
);
```

We have to import `./index.sass` in order to connect the stylesheet as a module to our system. All the styles will be rendered to the `/_next/static/style.css` file.

We have to add support for Sass to Next.js; this is done via `config`:

```
// next.config.js
const withSass = require('@zeit/next-sass')
module.exports = withSass()
```

Now, let's run the dev server:

```
$ npm start
```

If you open `http://localhost:3000` in the browser, you will see text styled as expected:

Another useful thing is the configuration of the `build/dev` phases via `custom config`.

To do that, you can use the following template:

```
// next.config.js
const withSass = require('@zeit/next-sass');

const {PHASE_DEVELOPMENT_SERVER} = require('next/constants');

module.exports = (phase, {defaultConfig}) => {

    if(phase === PHASE_DEVELOPMENT_SERVER) {
        return withSass(defaultConfig);
    }

    return withSass(Object.assign({}, defaultConfig, {
        distDir: 'build-custom'
    }));

};
```

In this example, we have added SASS support, along with more granular control over the production build. Here, we have set the destination directory to `build-custom`. The function receives `phase` and the `defaultConfig` as arguments, and you can use `phase` to determine what has to be modified in `defaultConfig`, based on your preferences.

Here, `config` also allows us to expose variables to your pages at runtime:

```
// next.config.js
module.exports = {
  serverRuntimeConfig: {
    serverOnly: 'secret' // no special meaning, just a hint that it's not
visible at the client
  },
  publicRuntimeConfig: {
    serverAndClient: 'public' // this will be visible on client
  }
};
```

You may use them as follows:

```
// pages/index.js
import React from 'react';
import getConfig from 'next/config'
import "./index.sass";

const {serverRuntimeConfig, publicRuntimeConfig} = getConfig();
```

```
console.log({serverRuntimeConfig, publicRuntimeConfig});

export default () => (
    <div>
        Styled text
        <pre>{JSON.stringify(serverRuntimeConfig, null, 2)}</pre>
        <pre>{JSON.stringify(publicRuntimeConfig, null, 2)}</pre>
    </div>
);
```

One potential use of this pattern is to hide some server-specific variables such as access tokens or anything sensitive. Two separate sections of config give a clear understanding of its visibility.

Now, restart the dev server, open the browser and console, and load `http://localhost:3000`; you will see the following:

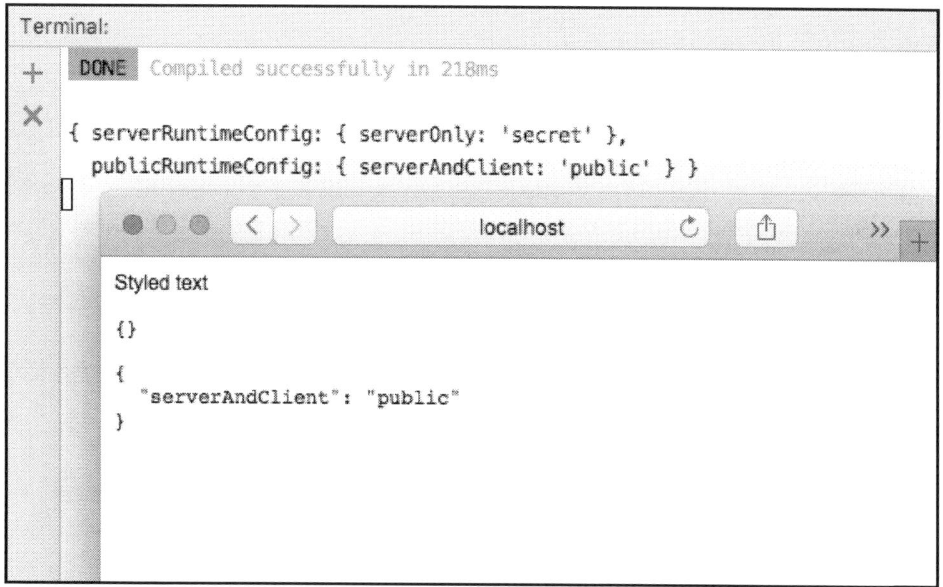

As you can see in the screenshot, both variables are defined in terminal output (on the server), but only the public one is defined on the client.

Configuring Webpack

Webpack is the bundler used to produce the Next.js dev server and builds. It can be configured to bundle more things than by default. As an example, let's add TypeScript.

Create `tsconfig.json`:

```
{
  "compileOnSave": false,
  "compilerOptions": {
    "allowSyntheticDefaultImports": true,
    "baseUrl": ".",
    "jsx": "preserve",
    "lib": [
      "dom",
      "es2015",
      "es2016"
    ],
    "module": "esnext",
    "moduleResolution": "node",
    "sourceMap": true,
    "skipLibCheck": true,
    "target": "esnext",
    "typeRoots": [
      "./node_modules/@types"
    ]
  }
}
```

We need to install the required packages (loader, compiler, and typings):

```
$ npm install ts-loader@3 typescript @types/react @types/next --save-dev
```

As of Next 5.0.1, TS Loader should be from the 3.x branch, because Next works on Webpack 3.

Next, modify the `config`:

```
module.exports = {
  webpack(config, {dir, defaultLoaders}) {
    config.module.rules.push({ // add a custom loader rule
      test: /\.+(ts|tsx)$/, // apply this rule only to TS[X] files
      use: [
        defaultLoaders.babel, // we use default babel on top of TS
        {
```

```
            loader: 'ts-loader',
            options: {transpileOnly: true}
          }
        ],
        include: [dir],
        exclude: /node_modules/ // exclude everything from node_modules for
performance
      });
      config.resolve.extensions.push('.ts', '.tsx'); // register require
resolve extensions
      return config;
    }
};
```

Rename your `pages/index.js` to `pages/index.tsx` and leave the contents as is; JS is a valid TS as well.

Now, since we know how to do it from the ground up, let's take a look at some established practices, for example via a plugin:

```
$ npm install @zeit/next-typescript @types/react @types/next --save-dev
```

Then, your `next.config.js` will look a lot simpler:

```
const withTypescript = require('@zeit/next-typescript');
module.exports = withTypescript({});
```

Configuring Babel

This is actually really simple. Next.js comes with a pre-baked preset for Babel, so you can simply create `.babelrc` and put in the following:

```
{
  "presets": ["next/babel"],
  "plugins": []
}
```

This may be useful, for example, for tests; keep this config if you'd like to use Jest, for instance:

```
{
  "presets": [
    "next/babel",
    "env"
  ],
  "env": {
```

```
        "test": {
          "presets": [
            "next/babel",
            ["env", {"modules": "commonjs"}]
          ]
        }
      }
    }
```

Here, we are using Babel's ability to have a different set of plugins and presets based on environment.

You will also need to install `babel-preset-env`:

```
$ npm install babel-preset-env --save-dev
```

We will talk more about tests in the next chapters.

Summary

In this chapter, we learned more advanced configurations of Next.js. Using this knowledge, we can now add more sophisticated build scenarios and extend the default functionality, such as with additional Webpack loaders and features, as well as custom Babel plugins and presets.

4
Next.js Data Flow

This is an extremely important chapter, which explains the purpose of all JS applications: talking to the backend. We will explain different approaches, including vanilla Next.js flow, with no frameworks, which is useful for understanding the essence of interaction. Then, we dive deeper into more and more advanced solutions.

This chapter covers the following:

- What's the difference between loading data on the client and on the server?
- Loading data using Vanilla JS
- Redux
- GraphQL and Relay
- Apollo GraphQL

Nuances of fetching data on the client and on the server

Servers and clients have different libraries that allow you to load data. In the browser, there are `XMLHttpRequest` and `WhatWG` Fetch API, and, on the server side, there are the Node.js default `http` and `https` packages. In order to load data universally (such as in an isomorphic manner,both on the server and on the client, using the same code base), we need to install an additional network layer.

There are two options here:

1. The first option is to simply polyfill the WhatWG Fetch API, since it's natively available on the client side in browsers.

   In order to do that, we should install a package:

   ```
   $ npm install isomorphic-fetch --save
   ```

And then, we require/import it anywhere before `fetch()` usages:

```
import 'isomorphic-fetch';

(async () => {
    const res = await fetch(...); // already polyfilled
})();
```

2. Another way is to use a universal library that will take care of the network layer; for example, the most popular one is Axios:

```
$ npm install axios --save
```

Then, we can use it right away after importing it:

```
import axios from 'axios';

(async () => {
    const res = await axios.get(...);
})();
```

This approach gives more control by using Axios configuration.

Loading data from a remote server using vanilla Next.js

Let's begin with a quick explanation of how data is usually loaded in traditional React apps.

If you don't use any data management frameworks, then your best bet is to request data when the component will mount, as shown here:

```
class Foo extends React.Component {

  state = {data: null};

  loadData = async () => await (await fetch('...')).json();

  async componentWillMount(){
    const data = await this.loadData();
    this.setState({data});
  }

  render(){
    if (!this.state.data) return (<div>Loading...</div>);
    return (<pre>{JSON.stringify(this.state.data)}</pre>);
```

```
    }

  }
```

This will initiate the data loading process when the component is about to be mounted. Before the data is made available, it will show a loading indicator.

Unfortunately, this will not work in a server environment during server-side rendering, because the server will not know that it should wait for data to arrive, so it will always send the "Loading" state to the client, and obviously this ruins the whole idea of SSR.

Next.js, of course, comes with a *very* handy method for that, a static method called `getInitialProps()`:

```
class Foo extends React.Component {

  static loadData = async () => await (await fetch('...')).json();

  async static getInitialProps(){
    const data = await this.loadData();
    return {data};
  }


  render(){
    if (!this.props.data) return (<div>Loading...</div>);
    return (<pre>{JSON.stringify(this.props.data)}</pre>);
  }

}
```

But this is too simplistic. Most likely, we will have to fetch based on certain conditions, such as a given ID or something else.

This has also been taken care of by Next.js.

Assume that we have something like this in the server code:

```
server.get('/post/:id', (req, res) => {
    const actualPage = '/second';
    const queryParams = {id: req.params.id};
    app.render(req, res, actualPage, queryParams);
});
```

Let's modify the data-related code to handle those IDs:

```
class Foo extends React.Component {

  static loadData = async (id) => await (await fetch('...')).json();

  async static getInitialProps(context){
    const {id} = context.query;
    const data = await this.loadData(id);
    return {data};
  }


  render(){
    if (!this.props.data) return (<div>Loading...</div>);
    return (<pre>{JSON.stringify(this.props.data)}</pre>);
  }

}
```

Using Redux with Next.js

The vast majority of traditional UI apps use the MVC pattern to organize state management. But in real-time client-side apps, this also quickly becomes a pain because models need to be synchronized, state is scattered, and there is no single source of truth. Different models can influence other models and the situation quickly gets out of hand. Another issue is bidirectional data flow between view and model (through the controller), where the view calls some controller method, which in turn calls a model method, which causes other models to update, then the updated state is passed back to the view.

In order to overcome this, the FLUX ideology was created. In this ideology, the direction of data/event propagation is constant; **View** does not communicate back and forth with the model. Instead, view issues **Action** and **Dispatcher** pick up those actions to update necessary **Stores**, which returns the data back to views. This decouples views from the rest of the data handling infrastructure:

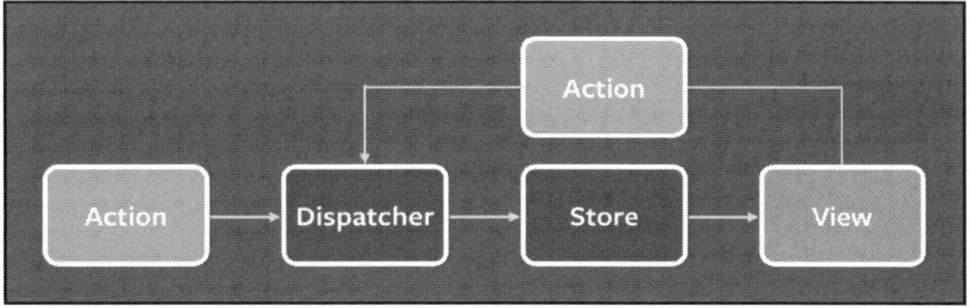

Let's illustrate a FLUX-inspired architecture based only on React:

```
class TopLevelStateContainer extends React.Component {
    state = {currentUser: null}; // let's pretend that this data is a
curren
    loadUser = () => (...);
    render(){
        return (<IntermediateComponent {...this.state}
loadUser={this.loadUser} />);
    }
}

// this could be a top menu bar
const IntermediateComponent = (props) => (
    <div>
         ...some additional markup and functionality
         <LoggedUserAvatar {...props}/>
    </div>
);

// this is the component that actually needs the data and a mutator/loader
function
class LoggedUserAvatar extends React.Component {
    componentWillMount(){
        this.props.loadUser();
    }
    render(){
        return (
            <div>{this.props.currentUser}</div>
        );
    }
}
```

The bad thing about this particular example is the necessity to pass the state and state mutators everywhere in the app including the components that should not even be aware of such things. As you can see in this example, `IntermediateComponent` has to pass the data and loader to `LoggedUserAvatar`, but it does not use it, so this is unnecessary knowledge. This will further lead to more and more edits if we need to update a leaf component or a top-level component.

Also, the state of the app cannot be snapshotted and persisted between app launches (such as when the page is reloaded). If there will be a ton of such leaf components that reuse the same sections of the top-level state, it will lead to a nightmare with the synchronization of access, interaction with such state, and so on.

There are plenty of different state management tools available for React, but one of the most popular is Redux. Redux is a predictable state container for JavaScript apps, not limited to only React ones, which plays perfectly with FLUX's unidirectional data flow and React's functional nature.

Redux consists of a store that has the main app state, a set of connected components that listen to changes in that state, a number of actions (objects that describe a change), and reducers (functions that mutate the state according to an action).

Let's take a deeper look into all of this.

As usual, we start with installation:

```
npm install redux react-redux --save
```

As we just learned, when Next.js renders pages, it takes files located in the `./pages` directory, takes `default export`, and uses the `getInitialProps` static method (which could also be asynchronous) to provide a props component. For consistency, this method is called on both the backend and frontend with one important remark: it will not be called on the frontend if it was called on the backend previously. The method receives a normalized `pathname` and `query` as parameters in both backend and frontend use, along with `req` (Node.js Request) on the server side.

So in order to inject Redux into the life cycle, we want to dispatch actions from the `getInitialProps` function, wait for them to be finished (so that the render function will have access to the updated `state`), and then render the resulting HTML and send it along with the final `state` of the Redux `store`. Then, we will recover the `state` on the client side:

```
async getInitialProps({store}) {
  await store.dispatch({type: 'FOO', payload: 'foo'}); // this could be
async
  return {custom: 'custom'};
}
```

In order to properly plug in the Next.js life cycle, we will use a special wrapper component provided by Next.js. In this wrapper, we have to add a React Redux Provider, which will be accessible by all child components, including our pages. We will use **Higher Order Components** (**HOC**) to wrap the Next.js wrapper. For the record, HOC is a function that accepts a `Component` and returns a wrapped version of it, which is also a `Component`. Sometimes, an HOC can accept arguments and return another function, which in turn will take a `Component` as an argument.

Basically, this is a short explanation of how the `next-redux-wrapper` package works.

First, it has to be installed:

```
$ npm install next@6 next-redux-wrapper react react-dom redux react-redux -
-save
```

Next.js 6.x introduced a new technology, an `App` component that wraps all pages and can provide something to them.

We will attach them with a Redux wrapper of `next-redux-wrapper` to the `_app` component; all other pages and components can stay using the regular `connect` HOC of the `react-redux` package as usual:

```
// pages/_app.js
import React from "react";
import {createStore} from "redux";
import withRedux from "next-redux-wrapper";

const reducer = (state = {foo: ''}, action) => {
    switch (action.type) {
        case 'FOO':
            return {...state, foo: action.payload};
        default:
            return state;
    }
```

```
};

class MyApp extends React.Component {

    static async getInitialProps({Component, ctx}) {

        // we can dispatch something common for all pages from here
        ctx.store.dispatch({type: 'FOO', payload: 'foo'});

        if (Component.getInitialProps) return {pageProps: await
Component.getInitialProps};
        return {};

    }

    render() {
        const {Component, pageProps = {}} = this.props;
        return (
            <Component {...pageProps} />
        );
    }

}

export default withRedux(makeStore)(MyApp);
```

And then, the actual page components can simply be connected as usual:

```
// pages/index.js
import React, {Component} from "react";
import {connect} from "react-redux";

export default connect(
    (state) => ({foo: state.foo})
)(class extends Component {

    static getInitialProps({store, isServer, pathname, query}) {
        // dispatch page-specific actions
        store.dispatch({type: 'FOO', payload: 'foo'});
        // pass custom props to page
        return {custom: 'custom'};
    }

    render() {
        return (
            <div>
                <div>Prop from Redux {this.props.foo}</div>
                <div>Prop from getInitialProps {this.props.custom}</div>
```

```
            </div>
        )
    }

});
```

You can see the full example in the Next.js repo at `https://github.com/zeit/next.js/blob/master/examples/with-redux/README.md` or check out the main repo's example here: `https://github.com/kirill-konshin/next-redux-wrapper/blob/master/pages/index.js`.

Here is a quick tip about authentication. We may store authentication anywhere in the app, but since we are using Redux, it makes sense to put this state-related data there too. Here is a way to use tokens from the Redux state for API requests.

Let's install middleware:

```
$ npm install redux-thunk redux-promise-middleware --save
```

Now, let's use them:

```
import {applyMiddleware, createStore} from "redux";
import thunkMiddleware from "redux-thunk";
import promiseMiddleware from "redux-promise-middleware";
import {request} from "./lib";
import reducers from "./reducers";

export default (initialState, options) => {

    let store;

    const api = (request) => {

        const {url, ...init} = request;
        let res = fetch(url, { // this is some library that makes requests
            ...init,
            headers: {
                Authorization: 'Bearer ' + store.getState().token // here
goes your
                selector
            }
        });

        // service action to enable reducers to capture HTTP errors
        // we can combine it with "if (res.ok) ..." to only dispatch on
errors
        store.dispatch({
```

```
            type: 'HTTP',
            payload: res,
            meta: request
        });

        return res;

    };

    store = createStore(
        reducers,
        initialState,
        applyMiddleware(
            thunkMiddleware.withExtraArgument(api),
            promiseMiddleware()
        )
    );

    return store;

};
```

Using promise middleware, we may `dispatch` promises as payloads, so we can directly use the API assigned at thunk middleware to send requests to the backend:

```
export const load = (id) => (dispatch, getState, api) => dispatch({
    type: 'LOAD',
    payload: api({url: `/something/${id}`})
});
```

In the reducer, you can now invalidate (for example remove) the token on HTTP 401 errors:

```
import {combineReducers} from "redux";

const isHttpAuthError = (payload) => (
    payload && payload.response && payload.response.status === 401
);

const token = (state = '', {type, payload}) => {
    switch (type) {
        case ('HTTP_REJECTED'):
            return (isHttpAuthError(payload)) ? null : state;
        // other token-related cases
        default:
            return state;
    }
};
```

```
export default combineReducers({
  token
});
```

Using GraphQL with Next.js to fetch data

In this chapter, we will learn how to use basic GraphQL with the Relay framework. But first, let's briefly talk about why GraphQL was introduced and what issues it solves.

When dealing with REST APIs, it is quite common to make some subsequent requests, for example, to get some entities and then for those entities get more sub-entities. By definition, REST endpoints should only provide one type of entity, and any thing else should be fetched from other endpoints, either by following HATEOAS links or by manually creating sub-requests. This increases the amount of network traffic, which forces all clients to re-implement logic for which sub-entities should be fetched and how, and badly affects the overall user interface. Of course, we can break the rules and put nested entities right there inside the API endpoint, but what if we have more than one level of nesting? Plus, what if we don't need some of the fields at all? Why should the server perform expensive data fetching and processing if the client only needs a fraction of this data?

In order to overcome these REST drawbacks, a new approach called GraphQL was created. It allows us to statically describe all relationships between different entities and then describe a query that could be used to download everything the client needs in one piece, no matter how deep the nesting. It also allows us to describe the specific fields the client requires.

The philosophy of GraphQL and React brings us to the idea that components can express their data needs by using GraphQL queries that will be picked up by a framework, and the resulting data will be injected into components when it is available.

In this chapter, we will try to stay as close as possible to the reference implementation by Facebook; in the next chapter, we will also take a look at what other tools are available on the market:

1. First of all, we will have to install a few packages:

```
$ npm install --save-dev babel-plugin-relay graphql-cli relay-compiler
```

2. Then, let's configure the GraphQL environment by putting the `.graphqlconfig` file in the project root:

```
{
  "schemaPath": "data/schema.graphql",
  "extensions": {
    "endpoints": {
      "dev": "https://swapi.graph.cool"
    }
  }
}
```

3. Now, we can download the schema locally. This is needed in order to enable the ahead-of-time optimizations that can be done by the Relay framework. In order to download the schema, we will create an npm script in `package.json`:

```
{
  "scripts": {
    "schema": "graphql get-schema"
  }
}
```

4. Now, if we run this:

```
$ npm run schema
```

5. We will see that the schema has been downloaded into `data/schema.grapql`, as stated in the config.
6. Our code base will query the GraphQL API endpoint using specially defined queries. In order to parse those queries ahead of time, we will create another script:

```
{
  "scripts": {
    "relay": "relay-compiler --src ./pages/ --schema
data/schema.graphql"
  },
}
```

7. So far, there is nothing to parse yet, so let's create our first page. But before that, we need to set up Relay's runtime environment:

```
// components/environment.js
import 'isomorphic-fetch';
import {Environment, Network, RecordSource, Store} from 'relay-
runtime';
import config from 'json-loader!../.graphqlconfig';
```

```
const fetchQuery = async (operation, variables) => {

   const res = await fetch(config.extensions.endpoints.dev, {
       method: 'POST',
       headers: {
           'Content-Type': 'application/json'
        },
        body: JSON.stringify({
            query: operation.text,
            variables,
       }),
   });

    return await res.json();

};

let environment;

export const getEnviroment = (records) => {
     if (!environment || !process.browser) {
         environment = new Environment({
            network: Network.create(fetchQuery),
            store: new Store(new RecordSource(records)),
         });
   }
   return environment;
};

export default getEnviroment;
```

Here, via JSON loader we used the same GraphQL config as in the download script. We configured Fetch to load data from the API endpoint where the schema is deployed.

8. Now, we can import this environment and create our first GraphQL query:

```
import React from 'react';
import {graphql, QueryRenderer} from 'react-relay';
import getEnvironment from "../components/environment";

const query = graphql`
    query pagesFilmsQuery {
        allFilms {
            id,
            director,
            title,
            characters {
                name
```

```
            }
        }
    }
`;

const Films = ({error, allFilms = null}) => {

    if (error) return (
        <div>Error! {error.message}</div>
    );

    if (!allFilms) return (
        <div>Loading...</div>
    );

    return (
        <div>
            {allFilms.map(film => (
                <div key={film.id}>
                    <h1>{film.title}</h1>
                    <p>Director: {film.director}</p>
                    <p>Characters: {film.characters.map(c =>
c.name).join(', ')}</p>
                </div>
            ))}
        </div>
    );

};

const Index = ({props, records}) => (
    <div>
        <QueryRenderer
            environment={getEnvironment()}
            query={query}
            variables={{}}
            render={({error, props}) => (
                <Films error={error} allFilms={props && props.allFilms}/>
            )}
        />
    </div>
);

export default Index;
```

Here, we have created a query that will fetch `allFilms` with certain nested fields, such as `title`, `director`, and `names` of `characters`:

```
const query = graphql`
    query pagesFilmsQuery {
        allFilms {
            id,
            director,
            title,
            characters {
                name
            }
        }
    }
`;
```

9. Next, let's configure Babel to understand queries by putting the following in a `.babelrc`:

```
{
  "passPerPreset": true,
  "presets": [
    "next/babel"
  ],
  "plugins": [
    "relay"
  ]
}
```

As you can see, from the client perspective it's just one request; the server will take care of all the nested data relationships.

Now, if we run this:

```
$ npm run relay
```

We will compile this query into something runnable by the Relay framework at runtime. After that, we can finally launch Next.js and see the list loaded using GraphQL.

But if we change the query, it will not be picked up by the client, so let's change things a bit.

First, let's install a tool that allows us to run two npm scripts in parallel:

```
$ npm install npm-run-all --save-dev
```

And then, let's create a slightly different set of scripts:

```
{
  "scripts": {
    "start:next": "next",
    "start:replay": "npm run relay -- --watch",
    "start": "npm run schema && npm-run-all -p start:*",
    "schema": "graphql get-schema",
    "relay": "relay-compiler --src ./pages/ --schema data/schema.graphql"
  }
}
```

Now, if we run this:

```
$ npm start
```

It will first download a fresh schema (if there are any), then run the schema compiler and Next.js in parallel, which guarantees that all changes will be included in the resulting build.

Unfortunately, `QueryRenderer` is not quite aware of Next.js and so it is rendered only on the client. If we'd like to use `GraphQL` on the server too, we need to alter the way our query is executed:

```
import React from 'react';
import {fetchQuery, graphql, QueryRenderer} from 'react-relay';
import getEnvironment from "../components/environment";

const query = graphql`
    query pagesFilmsQuery {
        allFilms {
            id,
            director,
            title,
            characters {
                name
            }
        }
    }
`;

const Films = ({error, allFilms = null}) => {

    if (error) return (
        <div>Error! {error.message}</div>
    );

    if (!allFilms) return (
        <div>Loading...</div>
```

```
    );

    return (
        <div>
            {allFilms.map(film => (
                <div key={film.id}>
                    <h1>{film.title}</h1>
                    <p>Director: {film.director}</p>
                    <p>Characters: {film.characters.map(c =>
c.name).join(', ')}</p>
                </div>
            ))}
        </div>
    );

};

class Index extends React.Component {

    constructor(props, context){
        super(props, context);
        this.environment = getEnvironment(props.records);
    }

    render() {
        const {props, records} = this.props;
        return (
            <div>
                <Films allFilms={props.allFilms}/>
            </div>
        );
    }

}

Index.getInitialProps = async () => {
    const environment = getEnvironment();
    const props = await fetchQuery(environment, query, {});
    const records = environment.getStore().getSource().toJSON();
    return {
        props, records
    };
};

export default Index;
```

Here, we have used Relay's `fetchQuery` function inside the `getInitialProps` static method; this will first load all the data and then render the page completely, even on the server.

The code for `getEnvironment` and `getInitialProps/constructor` obviously could be extracted into a HOC/base class.

Using the Apollo framework with Next.js to fetch data

Notice the bulkiness of the previous example. Even if we do not take into account the client/server code, we still end up with an inconvenient build process. What if we could make an app that will not require any build steps, precompilation, Babel plugins, and so on?

Recently, the Apollo Framework has received a lot of traction, and of course it has integration with Next.js.

All we need to do is to install a few packages:

```
$ npm i apollo-link-http next-apollo react-apollo graphql-tag --save
```

Then, we need to create a preconfigured HOC that we will attach to our pages:

```
import {withData} from 'next-apollo'
import {HttpLink} from 'apollo-link-http'

const config = {
    link: new HttpLink({
        uri: 'https://swapi.graph.cool',
        opts: {
            credentials: 'same-origin'
        }
    })
};

export default withData(config);
```

And then, we can use this HOC in pages:

```
import React from 'react';
import {graphql} from 'react-apollo';
import gql from 'graphql-tag';
import withData from "../components/withData";
```

```
const query = gql`
    query {
        allFilms {
            id,
            director,
            title,
            characters {
                name
            }
        }
    }
`;

let Index = ({data: {loading, allFilms, error}}) => {

    if (error) return (
        <div>Error! {error.message}</div>
    );

    if (loading) return (
        <div>Loading...</div>
    );

    return (
        <div>
            {allFilms.map(film => (
                <div key={film.id}>
                    <h1>{film.title}</h1>
                    <p>Director: {film.director}</p>
                    <p>Characters: {film.characters.map(c =>
c.name).join(', ')}</p>
                </div>
            ))}
        </div>
    );

};

Index = graphql(query)(Index);
Index = withData(Index);

export default Index;
```

Everything else is happening behind the scenes. HOC takes care of the Next.js data life cycle; it finds all the queries that have to be run, waits till they are complete, and then releases the data:

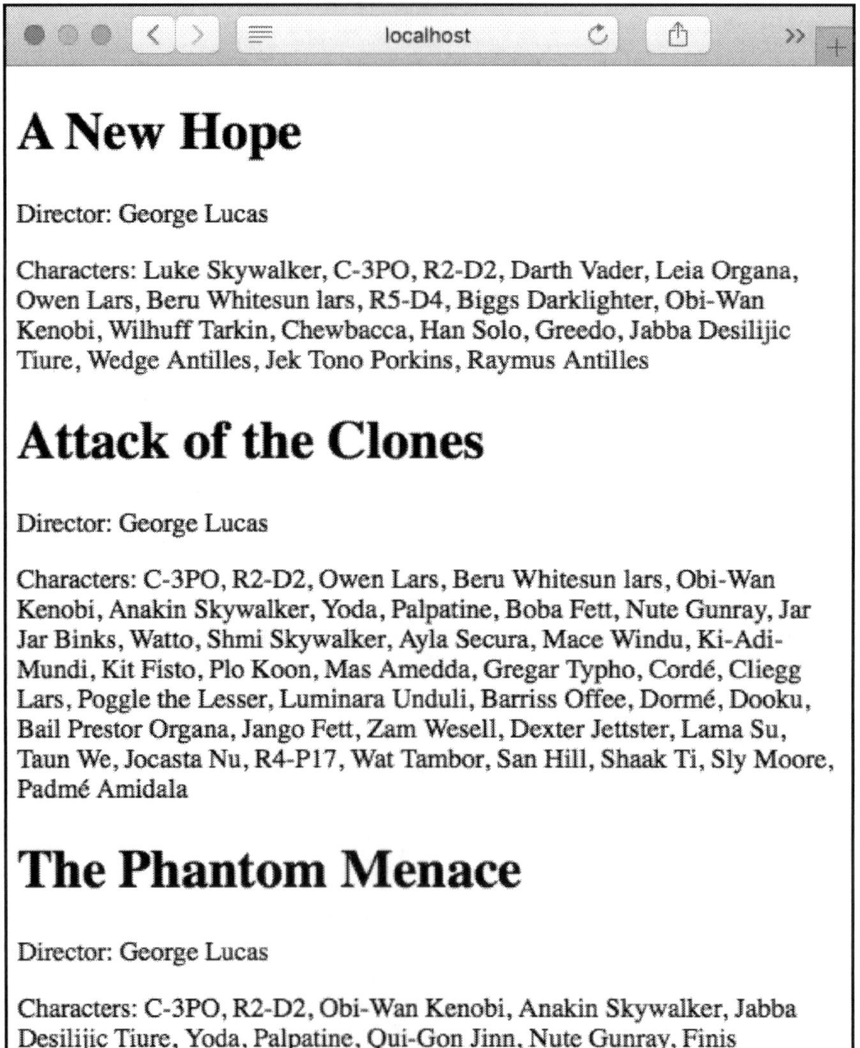

Summary

After reading this chapter, you should be capable of writing a fully functional application that can load data and manage its state. In the next chapter, we will cover more sophisticated topics about Next.js app patterns.

5
Application Life Cycle Handlers and Business Logic

Now, since we have learned all the basic stuff and we know how to use Next.js for everyday coding, we can move on to more complicated things, which are more about application architecture.

This chapter is not that much about Next.js, but it covers the most important and frequently asked questions about React-based app architecture and patterns. We explain how to design and implement the core concepts and more complex solutions:

- Authentication
- Role-based access control
- Business rule management
- Internationalization
- Error handling
- Caching
- Analytics

We explain these concepts and how to implement them in the Next.js world.

Authentication

Almost any application requires at least a very basic distinction between known users and guests, for example, to allow known users to store some of their information (such as their settings) in persistent storage on the backend side. It is quite obvious that users will want to access their data from anywhere, so we must fulfill this requirement.

Since the purpose of this book is a deep dive into Next.js, we will show how React and authentication best practices can be integrated specifically with Next.js.

But before we get started with the code, let's analyze the nature of the authentication process. It consists of several important aspects:

- Persistent storage of user credentials
- A method to send credentials to the server from the client side
- A check that finds the user and verifies the entered credentials
- A mechanism that signs all user requests so that the server can identify who is requesting what
- A mechanism that allows the user to sign out

For this example, we will take the static config of users, but API-wise we are going to build a system that should not care about the source of such data. For client-server interaction, we will use Redux and fetch as before. The check will be a simple function that verifies login and password. We will use cookies to sign requests as it's the simplest way to add something to all requests that go to the server.

Since we will be using custom server-side endpoints for login/logout, we will take the server example from an earlier chapter.

Let's start with the users server-side API. We will need a few packages:

```
$ npm install uuid lodash --save-dev
```

The idea of the login process will be quite straightforward: for each successful login attempt, we will create a UUID and attach it to the user so if this UUID is used to sign a request, we will be able to recover the user info from it.

Now, let's make the API:

```
const uuid = require('uuid/v4');
const find = require('lodash/find');

const users = [
    {username: 'admin', password: 'foo', group: 'admin'},
    {username: 'user', password: 'foo', group: 'user'},
];

const tokens = {};

const findUserByUsername = (username) => find(users, {username});

const findUserByToken = (token) => {
    if (!(token in tokens)) throw new Error('Token does not exist');
    return users[tokens[token]];
};
```

Here, we have created a static "DB"s of users and tokens. We have added two functions that allow us to find users by username and by token.

Now, let's use those function to perform the `login` procedure:

```
const login = (username, password) => {

    const user = findUserByUsername(username);

    if (!user) throw new Error('Cannot find user');

    if (user.password !== password) throw new Error('Wrong password');

    const token = uuid();

    tokens[token] = users.indexOf(user);

    return {
        token,
        user
    };

};
```

We attempt to find a user by username, and if that's successful, we compare the stored password and provided one. If this check is also successful, then we create a new token (UUID) and establish a relationship between token and user by creating an entry in the token storage. After that, we cut out sensitive user information and return the result.

Let's add the logout procedure:

```
const logout = (token) => {
    delete tokens[token];
};
```

This simple function deletes the token from storage; this makes sure that the token is useless and no users will be located based on it.

Here is the final API file:

```
// users.js
const uuid = require('uuid/v4');
const find = require('lodash/find');

const users = [
    {username: 'admin', password: 'foo', group: 'admin'},
    {username: 'user', password: 'foo', group: 'user'},
```

```
];

const tokens = {};

const findUserByUsername = (username) => find(users, {username});

const findUserByToken = (token) => {
    if (!(token in tokens)) throw new Error('Token does not exist');
    return users[tokens[token]];
};

const login = (username, password) => {

    const user = findUserByUsername(username);

    if (!user) throw new Error('Cannot find user');

    if (user.password !== password) throw new Error('Wrong password');

    const token = uuid();

    tokens[token] = users.indexOf(user);

    return {
        token,
        user
    };

};

const logout = (token) => {
    delete tokens[token];
};

exports.findUserByUsername = findUserByUsername;
exports.findUserByToken = findUserByToken;
exports.login = login;
exports.logout = logout;
```

We have to install a few packages to enable the request parsing functionality of Express:

```
$ npm install express body-parser cookie-parser --save-dev
```

Now, we can make the server:

```
// server.js
const express = require('express');
const next = require('next');
const bodyParser = require('body-parser');
const cookieParser = require('cookie-parser');

const port = 3000;
const cookieName = 'token';
const dev = process.env.NODE_ENV !== 'production';
const app = next({dev});
const handle = app.getRequestHandler();
const server = express();

server.use(cookieParser());

server.use(bodyParser.json());

server.get('*', (req, res) => {
    return handle(req, res);
});

app.prepare().then(() => {

    server.listen(port, (err) => {
        if (err) throw err;
        console.log('NextJS is ready on http://localhost:' + port);
    });

}).catch(e => {

    console.error(e.stack);
    process.exit(1);

});
```

Now, let's add an endpoint that will use an API method to log the user in, and if it's successful, it will set a cookie with the newly created token:

```
const cleanupUser = (user) => {
    const newUser = Object.assign({}, user);
    delete newUser.password;
    return newUser;
};

server.post('/api/login', (req, res) => {
```

```
    try {

        console.log('Attempting to login', req.body);

        const authInfo = users.login(req.body.username, req.body.password);
        authInfo.user = cleanupUser(authInfo.user);

        res.cookie(cookieName, authInfo.token, {
            expires: new Date(Date.now() + 1000 * 60 * 60 * 24),
            httpOnly: true
        });
        res.send(authInfo);

    } catch (e) {

        console.log('Login error', e.stack);

        res.status(400).send({message: 'Wrong username and/or password'});

    }
});
```

Now, let's add middleware that will help to figure out whether the user is authenticated and pull the user from the DB:

```
const authMiddleware = (dieOnError) => (req, res, next) => {
    req.user = null;
    req.token = null;
    try {
        req.token = req.cookies[cookieName];
        req.user = cleanupUser(users.findUserByToken(req.token));
        next();
    } catch (e) {
        if (dieOnError) {
            res.status(401).send({message: 'Not Authorized'});
        } else {
            next();
        }
    }
};
```

Next, we add a logout endpoint:

```
// note that we call authMiddleware with false in order to bypass the error
message sending
server.post('/api/logout', authMiddleware(false), (req, res) => {

    try {
```

```
        if (req.token) users.logout(req.token);
    } catch (e) {} // ignore errors

    res.clearCookie('token');
    res.send({});

});
```

Here, we simply call the API method to log out and clear the cookie because it's now useless.

Now the most intriguing part: how will we let the client know whether the user is authenticated or not? If it was a pure client-side app, we would have to call an API endpoint or access cookies on the client side (which is not secure; that's why we use HTTP-only cookies that are visible only to the server). But since we are using Next.js and server-side rendering, we can prepopulate user info right when the initial page is requested from the server.

To do that, we will add a few things to our Next.js endpoint:

```
server.get('*', authMiddleware(false), (req, res) => {
    // pass through everything to NextJS
    return handle(req, res);
});
```

Here, we try to use tokens from cookies to locate the user; if it's successful, it means user is authenticated, because otherwise the token would be wiped from storage, as was previously pointed out. Now, since we have located the user, we can put this info somewhere so that it will be accessible from Next.js. The perfect place for that is the `Request` object.

Here is the full server:

```
// server.js
const express = require('express');
const next = require('next');
const bodyParser = require('body-parser');
const cookieParser = require('cookie-parser');
const users = require('./users');

const port = 3000;
const cookieName = 'token';
const dev = process.env.NODE_ENV !== 'production';
const app = next({dev});
const handle = app.getRequestHandler();
const server = express();
```

```
const cleanupUser = (user) => {
    const newUser = Object.assign({}, user);
    delete newUser.password;
    return newUser;
};

server.use(cookieParser());

server.use(bodyParser.json());

server.post('/api/login', (req, res) => {

    try {

        console.log('Attempting to login', req.body);

        const authInfo = users.login(req.body.username, req.body.password);
        authInfo.user = cleanupUser(authInfo.user);

        res.cookie(cookieName, authInfo.token, {
            expires: new Date(Date.now() + 1000 * 60 * 60 * 24)}); //,
httpOnly: true
        res.send(authInfo);

    } catch (e) {

        console.log('Login error', e.stack);

        res.status(400).send({message: 'Wrong username and/or password'});

    }
});

const authMiddleware = (dieOnError) => (req, res, next) => {
    req.user = null;
    req.token = null;
    try {
        req.token = req.cookies[cookieName];
        req.user = cleanupUser(users.findUserByToken(req.token));
        next();
    } catch (e) {
        if (dieOnError) {
            res.status(401).send({message: 'Not Authorized'});
        } else {
            next();
        }
    }
};
```

```
server.post('/api/logout', authMiddleware(false), (req, res) => {

    try {
        if (req.token) users.logout(req.token);
    } catch (e) {} // ignore errors

    res.clearCookie('token');
    res.send({});

});

server.get('/api/me', authMiddleware(true), (req, res) => {
    res.send(req.user);
});

server.get('*', authMiddleware(false), (req, res) => {
    // pass through everything to NextJS
    return handle(req, res);
});

app.prepare().then(() => {

    server.listen(port, (err) => {
        if (err) throw err;
        console.log('NextJS is ready on http://localhost:' + port);
    });

}).catch(e => {

    console.error(e.stack);
    process.exit(1);

});
```

In order to access the user info, we will enhance Redux integration:

```
// lib/redux.js
import {applyMiddleware, createStore} from 'redux';
import thunk from 'redux-thunk';
import logger from 'redux-logger';

export const makeStore = (initialState, {isServer, req, debug, storeKey})
=> {
    if (isServer) {
        // only do it now bc on client it should be undefined by default
        initialState = initialState || {};
        // server has put things in req
        initialState.user = req.user;
```

```
        initialState.token = req.token;
        initialState.error = null;
    }
    return createStore(reducer, initialState, applyMiddleware(thunk,
logger));
};
```

When it is a server-side execution, we will take the info from the request and use it to prepopulate `initialState`. After that, the info will be immediately available in all `getInitialProps` methods and in connected components.

Now, let's add the required client-side methods to allow users to sign in and out. This is the reducer:

```
// lib/redux.js
const LOGIN_SUCCESS = 'LOGIN_SUCCESS';
const LOGIN_ERROR = 'LOGIN_ERROR';
const LOGOUT = 'LOGOUT';
const DEFAULT_STATE = {
    user: null,
    token: null,
    error: null
};

export const reducer = (state = DEFAULT_STATE, {type, payload}) => {
    switch (type) {
        case LOGIN_SUCCESS:
            return {
                ...state,
                ...DEFAULT_STATE,
                user: payload.user,
                token: payload.token
            };
        case LOGOUT:
            return {
                ...state,
                ...DEFAULT_STATE
            };
        case LOGIN_ERROR:
            return {
                ...state,
                ...DEFAULT_STATE,
                error: payload
            };
        default:
            return state
    }
};
```

Now, let's create actions that will call server API endpoints:

```
// lib/redux.js
const SERVER = 'http://localhost:3000';

const apiRequest = ({url, body = undefined, method = 'GET'}) =>
fetch(SERVER + url, {
    method,
    body: typeof body === 'undefined' ? body : JSON.stringify(body),
    headers: {'content-type': 'application/json'},
    credentials: 'include'
});

export const login = (username, password) => async (dispatch) => {
    try {
        const res = await apiRequest({
            url: '/api/login',
            body: {username, password},
            method: 'POST'
        });
        const json = await res.json();
        if (!res.ok) {
            dispatch({type: LOGIN_ERROR, payload: json.message});
            return;
        }
        dispatch({type: LOGIN_SUCCESS, payload: json});
    } catch (e) {
        dispatch({type: LOGIN_ERROR, payload: e.message});
    }
};

export const logout = () => async (dispatch) => {
    try {
        await apiRequest({
            url: '/api/logout',
            method: 'POST'
        });
    } catch (e) {}
    dispatch({type: LOGOUT});
};
```

Here, we use the `apiRequest` method to call the backend with parameter credentials = include which add cookies to request.

And now the final step, bringing it all together in a page that will render appropriate content based on user status:

```
import React from "react";
```

```
import {login, logout, me, makeStore} from "../lib/redux";
import withRedux from "next-redux-wrapper";

const Index = ({login, logout, me, user, error}) => (
    <div>
        {error && (<div>Login error: {error}</div>)}
        {(!!user ? (
            <div>
                <h1>Logged in as {user.username}</h1>
                <button onClick={() => me()}>Alert my info</button>
                <button onClick={() => logout()}>Logout</button>
            </div>
        ) : (
              <div>
                  <h1>Not logged in</h1>
                  <button onClick={() => login('admin',
'foo')}>Login</button>
                  {/* here we have hardcoded the user info because we don't
have a login form */}
              </div>
          ))}
    </div>
);

export default withRedux(
    makeStore,
    (state) => ({user: state.user, error: state.error}),
    {login, logout, me}
)(Index);
```

We have connected a page to Redux using the wrapper, and then in the `render()` method of the functional component, we accessed the user and error properties of state to understand the user status.

Now, if the user clicks the Login button, Redux will dispatch an action, which will send a request to the server, which will respond either with an error or with user information, which will be available in the store's state. If the user reloads the page, the same info will be injected by the server, based on the cookie.

As a further activity, we may now add more server-side API methods and protect them the same way as the logout endpoint:

```
// server.js
server.post('/api/me', authMiddleware(true), (req, res) => {
 res.send(req.user);
});
```

The Redux action for that will be as follows:

```
export const me = () => async (dispatch) => {
    // We don't dispatch anything for demo purposes only
    try {
        const res = await (await apiRequest({url: '/api/me'})).json();
        alert(JSON.stringify(res));
    } catch (e) {
        console.error(e.stack);
    }
};
```

Access Control List, Roles, and Permissions

In large apps, simple authentication with logged in and logged out checks is often not enough. Users may have different access levels, for example, admins and regular users, moderators and super admins. In addition to that, users may have different permissions on individual resources; for instance, a user can delete or edit their own blog post, but cannot do anything with someone else's post. Such complex permission and role-based systems can are usually called Role-Based Access Control (RBAC).

There are many open source implementations, but for our case we need a special one: it must be isomorphic because permissions checks will be performed both on the client and the server sides.

We will start with defining the RBAC. For this purpose, we will take the library called `accesscontrol` because it works both on the client and the server:

```
$ npm install accesscontrol --save
```

The library allows us to define roles, inherit roles, define resources, perform actions over them, and even access the properties of those resources.

We will not go super far into the definition. You can later update it up to your app requirements. We will focus more on the mechanics and the layer between RBAC and Next.js.

First, let's define the grants:

```
// lib/rbac.js
const accesscontrol = require('accesscontrol');

const ac = new accesscontrol.AccessControl({
    admin: {
```

```
        page: {
            'create:any': ['*'],
            'read:any': ['*'],
            'update:any': ['*'],
            'delete:any': ['*']
        }
    },
    user: {
        page: {
            'create:own': ['*'],
            'read:any': ['*'],
            'update:own': ['*'],
            'delete:own': ['*']
        }
    }
});

const checkGrant = (user, action, resource) => user ?
ac.can(user.group)[action](resource).granted : false;

exports.checkGrant = checkGrant;
```

We have to stick to `CommonJS` module notation since we will use this file as is on the Node.js server as well. Be careful with this approach and always pay attention so you don't drag unnecessary things into the server context.

Here, we have imported the main class from the `accesscontrol` package and configured all grants in bulk mode. This could also be done in a similar way if you store the config in a DB or elsewhere. Again, for simplicity and focus we will not go that far; a simple static config should be OK.

The config allows admins to do whatever they want with all posts, whereas users can only do actions with the posts that they have created.

Also, we have created a function that will check users' permissions to access a given resource.

Now, we need to make Next.js become aware of those grants and the very presence of access control. We will update the Redux Auth that we had before for that purpose.

Let's create a component.

This HOC assumes that it is used *after* `withRedux` because it is using a Redux store to get the user info:

```
// lib/withRedux.js
import React from "react";
```

```
import {connect} from "react-redux";

export default (checkCb) => (WrappedComponent) => {

    class WithRbac extends React.Component {

        static async getInitialProps(args) {

            const {user} = args.store.getState();

            // First time check
            const granted = checkCb(user);

            if (!granted && args.res) {
                args.res.statusCode = 401;
            }

            const additionalArgs = {...args, granted};

            return WrappedComponent.getInitialProps
                  ? await WrappedComponent.getInitialProps(additionalArgs)
                  : {};

        }

        render() {

            const granted = checkCb(this.props.user);

            // Runtime checks
            return (
                <WrappedComponent {...this.props} granted={granted}/>
            );

        }

    }

    WithRbac.displayName = `withRbac(${WrappedComponent.displayName
                                    || WrappedComponent.name
                                    || 'Component'})`;

    return connect(state => ({
        user: state.user
    }))(WithRbac);

}
```

This HOC works in two ways: on initial page render and at runtime. When the wrapped page is rendered for the first time, HOC takes user info from the Redux `store` and uses this info to check the grant. After that, it calls the page's `getInitialProps` method with additional grant info.

Runtime mode is required to properly handle status changes when the user signs in and out as part of SPA activity.

If the check was unsuccessful, HOC will return a suitable HTTP status.

Note that HOC does not depend on the RBAC module directly; it relies on whatever is passed to it as the check function `checkCb`. This is a good practice to untie modules and make them self-contained, and it will also be needed later.

Now, let's create some dummy data to be used in the demo page:

```
// lib/pages.js
export default [
    {
        user: 'admin',
        title: 'Page by Admin'
    },
    {
        user: 'user',
        title: 'Page by User'
    }
];
```

We have defined a few dummy posts and assigned a user for each post.

Now, let's use this data and HOC in the Next.js page:

```
// pages/index.js
import React from "react";
import {login, logout, makeStore} from "../lib/redux.js";
import withRedux from "next-redux-wrapper";
import withRbac from "../lib/withRbac";
import {checkGrant} from "../lib/rbac";
import pages from "../lib/pages";

let Index = ({login, logout, user, error, granted}) => (
    <div>
        {error && (<div>Login error: {error}</div>)}
        {(granted ? (
            <div>
                <h1>Logged in as {user.username}</h1>
                {pages.map((page, index) => (
```

```
                    <div key={index}>
                        {page.title}
                        {
                            checkGrant(
                                user,
                                (user.username === page.user ? 'updateOwn'
: 'updateAny'), 'page'
                            )
                            ? 'Can Write'
                            : 'Read Only'
                        }
                    </div>
                ))}
                <button onClick={() => logout()}>Logout</button>
            </div>
        ) : (
            <div>
                <h1>Not logged in</h1>
                <button onClick={() => login('admin', 'foo')}>Login
Admin</button>
                <button onClick={() => login('user', 'foo')}>Login
User</button>
            </div>
        ))}
    </div>
);

Index = withRbac(user => checkGrant(user, 'readAny', 'page'))(Index);
Index = withRedux(
    makeStore,
    (state) => ({
        user: state.user,
        error: state.error
    }),
    {login, logout}
)(Index);

export default Index;
```

Unlike in the simple auth example, we no longer rely on the presence of user info to determine page availability. Now, we can use the grant info in the `granted` variable to display appropriate content; moreover, we can use the `checkGrant` method to dynamically check any permissions at runtime.

Now, since we have everything in place, we can also add a check to the server API:

```
// server.js
const rbac = require('./lib/rbac');

const rbacMiddleware = (action, resource) => (req, res, next) => {
    if (rbac.checkGrant(req.user, action, resource)) {
        next();
    } else {
        res.status(403).send({message: 'Not enough permissions'});
    }
};

authServer.server.post('/api/rbac', authServer.authMiddleware(true),
rbacMiddleware('readAny', 'page'), (req, res) => {
    res.send({foo: 'bar'}); // whatever your API has to return
});
```

Business Rules Engine

Business Rules Engine is a technology (or pattern) for resolving specific user/system/permission/language-related conditions. It provides a convenient way to understand feature availability for the brand, account, or particular user, without knowing which actual conditions are involved in the check.

Why is such an API needed?

In order to better understand the approach, take a look at this JSX example:

```
<div>
    {(user.isAdmin && account.balance > 0) && (
        <button>Add users</button>
    )}
</div>
```

Obviously, these UI conditions are trying to figure out some specifics of the current state of the account and understand whether an action is permitted or not. Imagine now that under some other system conditions (the account is a trial, for example), there is no such case as balance; this system state has something a bit different instead of balance:

```
<div>
    {(user.isAdmin && (account.balance > 0 || account.isTrial)) && (
        <button>Add users</button>
    )}
</div>
```

As you can see, the conditional statement begins to grow and is bloated with logic and magic numbers.

One obvious solution is to introduce a certain level of abstraction, at least for the balance part. The business rules engine approach takes this even further:

```
<div>
    {(userBL.isAddUsersPermitted(user, account)) && (
        <button>Add users</button>
    )}
</div>
```

The whole complexity of the condition is hidden behind an abstract method that gives an answer to certain questions.

Inside of the API, anything may happen, new conditions may be added, removed, or reassembled in different ways, but the UI will not know about it unless the interface is changed.

We can call this API the Business Layer for simplicity and for naming purposes. I strongly suggest you have all such business logic-related things grouped together under one folder.

Some of the key principles are:

- **API consists of pure functions**: Based on the single responsibility principle, the API methods should not have side effects (for instance, they should not load data, store intermediate state, or cache anything; they should only depend on arguments). You can create an extra layer on top of this one, which will be capable of loading data and caching.
- **API is business feature-oriented**: The ability to add users is a feature, so there has to be a method for that called `isAddUserAvailable()`; naming it `showAddButton()` is inappropriate because it brings the UI context into business context.
- **Use of API methods should not be combined in the UI**: `brand.isA() && brand.isB()` is inappropriate; usage may be only a direct function call. If this situation occurs, it is a sign that BL should be updated because it is another business case/feature.
- **API provides granular and complex methods**: Internally, API methods must reuse other more granular methods in order to be always clean, self-explanatory, and understandable. Appropriate methods should be used according to the context of usage.

- **Initial configuration can be DI'ed into the constructor**: The only thing that could be injected and stored inside BL is the initial account/system configuration, and only if it is static and never changes between full page reloads, or if your system can reload it on demand.
- **Real-time data must not be a part of initial configuration**: All data should be provided; BL cannot load any data by itself.

Let's code now. We will reuse the previous chapter code and enhance it.

Let's create a module for business rules:

```
// ./lib/bl.js
import {checkGrant} from "./rbac";

export const canWritePost = (user, post) =>
    checkGrant(user, (user.username == post.user ? 'updateOwn' :
'updateAny'), 'page');

export const canReadPages = (user) =>
    checkGrant(user, 'readAny', 'page');
```

We have reused the `checkGrant` function from the RBAC module, so now we can clean up a page's code to make it more self-documenting and obvious:

```
// pages/index.js
import React from "react";
import {login, logout, makeStore} from "../lib/redux";
import withRedux from "next-redux-wrapper";
import withRbac from "../lib/withRbac";
import pages from "../lib/pages";
import {canReadPages, canWritePost} from "../lib/bl";

let Index = ({login, logout, user, error, granted}) => (
    <div>
        {error && (<div>Login error: {error}</div>)}
        {(granted ? (
            <div>
                <h1>Logged in as {user.username}</h1>
                {pages.map((page, index) => (
                    <div key={index}>
                        {page.title} - {canWritePost(user, page) ? 'Can
Write' : 'Read
                         Only'}
                    </div>
                ))}
                <button onClick={() => logout()}>Logout</button>
            </div>
```

```
        ) : (
                <div>
                    <h1>Not logged in</h1>
                    <button onClick={() => login('admin', 'foo')}>Login
Admin</button>
                    <button onClick={() => login('user', 'foo')}>Login
User</button>
                </div>
            ))}
    </div>
);

Index = withRbac(user => canReadPages(user))(Index);
Index = withRedux(
    makeStore,
    (state) => ({
        user: state.user,
        error: state.error
    }),
    {login, logout}
)(Index);

export default Index;
```

As you can see, now the page does not even know what the logic is behind the scenes, it just calls methods and provides the data needed to make a decision. It does not even depend on the RBAC module anymore, only on HOCs and BL, which means we can change the implementation and complexity of business rules at any time, and the page code will still use the same functions.

For pushing things further, we can load the permissions data from the server before calling the BL methods.

Internationalization and Localization

Any big app inevitably will have to be localized in order to widen the audience that can use the app. Besides using localized strings in the app, we also need to present dates and time in local format, and also might want to use pluralization for more human-readable messages. For date and time, the champion is MomentJS, and for pluralization, the ICU format is the most advanced one, so we picked Format Message as the library for that.

Here, we will show only one of the potential ways to localize the application. Next.js again brings some nuances because of its universal nature, so the way we have chosen fits perfectly for both client and server counterparts; for this example, we will use the I18Next library.

Let's install a few packages as usual; `isomorphic-unfetch` is needed since we will make `fetch` requests from the server too:

```
$ npm install i18next react-i18next isomorphic-unfetch moment format-
message --save
```

Then, we create the language files using the following directory structure convention:

```
/static
  /locales
    /en
      namespace.json
    /es
      namespace.json
```

Namespace here can be anything; we suggest using some domain-related namespaces.

We are using a static directory because these files will be loaded at runtime as simple JSON.

Let's put the translations in place:

```
// static/locales/en/common.json
{
  "HELLO": "Hello!",
  "BACK": "Back",
  "OTHER_PAGE": "Other page",
  "MESSAGES": "{count, plural, =0 {No unread messages} one {# unread
message} other {# unread messages}}"
}

// static/locales/en/other.json
{
  "GOOD_MORNING": "Good Morning!"
}

// static/locales/es/common.json
{
  "HELLO": "Hola!",
  "BACK": "Atrás",
  "OTHER_PAGE": "Otra página",
  "MESSAGES": "{count, plural, =0 {Sin mensajes no leídos} one {# mensaje no
leído} other {# mensajes no leídos}}"
}
```

```
// static/locales/es/other.json
{
  "GOOD_MORNING": "Buenos días!"
}
```

Now, let's create a HOC for top-level pages. We begin with a function that will allow us to load and store the translations:

```
// lib/withI18n.js
const baseUrl = 'http://localhost:3000/static/locales';
const getLangUrl = (lang, ns) => `${baseUrl}/${lang}/${ns}.json`;
let translation = null;

export const getTranslation = async (lang, namespaces) => {

    translation = translation || {}; //TODO Invalidate in dev mode

    for (let ns of namespaces) {

        if (!translation[lang] || !translation[lang][ns]) {

            let response = await fetch(getLangUrl(lang, ns));

            if (!response.ok) {
                response = await fetch(getLangUrl(fallbackLng, ns));
            }

            translation[lang] = translation[lang] || {};
            translation[lang][ns] = await response.json();
        }

    }

    return translation;

};
```

Here, we will be storing all namespaces of all locales in a module variable; this will prevent the script from loading them again and again (we assume that locales don't change often, but in reality there also should be a method to invalidate, at least in dev mode).

Now, let's create a HOC itself:

```
// lib/withI18n.js
import React from "react";
import i18n from 'i18next';
import {I18nextProvider, translate} from 'react-i18next'
import moment from 'moment';
```

```
import formatMessage from 'format-message';

const getLang = (cookie) => cookie.match(/lang=([a-z]+)/)[1];

export default (namespaces = []) => (WrappedComponent) => (

    class WithI18n extends React.Component {

        static displayName = `withI18n(${WrappedComponent.displayName
                                        || WrappedComponent.name
                                        || 'Component'})`;

        static async getInitialProps(args) {

            const req = args.req;

            const lng = (req && req.headers.cookie &&
getLang(req.headers.cookie))
                        || (document && getLang(document.cookie))
                        || fallbackLng;

            const resources = await getTranslation(
                lng,
                [defaultNS, ...namespaces] // list other namespaces here
when needed
            );

            const props = WrappedComponent.getInitialProps
                          ? await WrappedComponent.getInitialProps(args)
                          : {};

            return {
                ...props,
                resources,
                lng
            };

        }

        constructor(props, context) {

            super(props, context);

            const {lng, resources} = props;

            translation = translation || resources; // recover client side
cache of
            translations
```

```
            this.i18n = i18n.init({
                fallbackLng,
                lng,
                resources,
                defaultNS,
                ns: [defaultNS],
                debug: false
            });

            // this allows to use translation in pages
            this.Wrapper = translate(namespaces)(WrappedComponent);

            this.moment = moment().locale(lng);

        }

        render() {

            const {Wrapper, moment, props: {resources, ...props}} = this;

            return (
                <I18nextProvider i18n={this.i18n}>
                    <Wrapper {...props} moment={moment}
msg={formatMessage}/>
                </I18nextProvider>
            );

        }

    }

);
```

Let's take a closer look at what is happening here. We begin with Next.js `getInitialProps` as always; there, we attempt to get current locale from cookies (by using different approaches for server and client with a fallback if we cannot determine it). Once the locale has been figured out, we load appropriate namespaces and return props. After that, in the component constructor (which is called for each page), we initialize an instance of the I18Next library with the `resources` received from `getInitialProps`. Then, we create a translated (wrapped) version of `WrappedComponent` so that the translation will be available on the page level too. Along with this, we also configure a moment instance too. Then, in the render, we wrap the wrapper (sic!) in an I18Next provider that will allow us to use translation in JSX and supply the `moment` and `formatMessage` instances.

Let's create two components, one for each namespace, for illustration purposes:

```
// components/Common.js
import React from "react";
import {translate} from 'react-i18next'

const Common = ({t}) => (
    <div>Component common: {t('HELLO')}</div>
);

export default translate()(Common);
```

This component is using the default namespace (common) and is very straightforward:

```
// components/other.js
import React from 'react'
import {translate} from 'react-i18next'

const Other = ({t}) => (
    <div>
        Component other: {t('other:GOOD_MORNING')}
    </div>
);

export default translate(['other'])(Other);
```

This component is using the `other` namespace; there is one very important remark about using custom namespaces in components, and we will talk about it further.

Now, let's create a page:

```
// pages/index.js
import React from 'react';
import Link from 'next/link';
import Common from '../components/Common';
import Other from '../components/Other';
import withI18n from '../lib/withI18n';

const setLocale = (lang) => {
    document.cookie = 'lang=' + lang + '; path=/';
    window.location.reload();
};

const getStyle = (current, lang) => ({fontWeight: current === lang ? 'bold'
: 'normal'});

const Index = ({t, lng, moment, msg}) => (
    <div>
```

```
            <div>Page-level common: {t('common:HELLO')}</div>
            <Common/>
            <Other/>
            <div>{moment.format('LLLL')}</div>
            <div>{msg(t('common:MESSAGES'), {count: 0})}</div>
            <div>{msg(t('common:MESSAGES'), {count: 1})}</div>
            <div>{msg(t('common:MESSAGES'), {count: 2})}</div>
            <Link href='/other'>
                <button>{t('common:OTHER_PAGE')}</button>
            </Link>
            <hr/>
            <button onClick={() => setLocale('en')} style={getStyle(lng,
'en')}>EN</button>
            <button onClick={() => setLocale('es')} style={getStyle(lng,
'es')}>ES</button>
            <button onClick={() => setLocale('de')} style={getStyle(lng,
'de')}>DE</button>
        </div>
);

export default withI18n()(Index);
```

In this page, we use the HOC that we just created with the default namespace (nothing is set). As per the HOC interface, we receive `t`, `lng`, `moment`, and `msg` as props. In order to change the locale, we set the cookie and reload the page.

Also, let's create a page for the `other` namespace:

```
// pages/other.js
import React from 'react';
import Link from 'next/link';
import Common from '../components/Common';
import Other from '../components/Other';
import withI18n from '../lib/withI18n';

const OtherPage = ({t}) => (
    <div>
        <div>Page-level other: {t('other:GOOD_MORNING')}</div>
        <Common/>
        <Other/>
        <Link href='/'>
            <button>{t('common:BACK')}</button>
        </Link>
    </div>

);

export default withI18n(['other'])(OtherPage);
```

Notice that we supply the `other` namespace to the HOC. Other than that it works exactly the same.

Now, about the important remark. If you open the Index page directly, you will notice that the Other component was not translated. This happened because the index page does not explicitly request the `other` namespace. But if you visit the Other page, everything will work as expected, translations will be loaded, and all components will be shown the way they should. But, there's more. If you first open the `Other` page and then click the "Back" button to return to the "Index" page, you will see that Other component is now translated. It happens because the `other` namespace was cached after the `Other` page visit. This means that you should explicitly request all necessary namespaces for both the page and all underlying components, which can be tricky sometimes. Our recommendation is to use some intermediate HOC for components to preload translations and then pass through, but keep in mind that the server will wait only for `fetch` inside the `getInitialProps` of pages, so consider this as a limitation of server-side rendering.

Error handling

Any application is prone to runtime errors. These could be various kinds of errors: caused by bugs, unexpected input, validation errors, poor network connectivity, or server errors. Lots of them. A well-designed app must not silently stop working or display an ugly error message with tons of irrelevant technical information. Instead, it must always display some meaningful error information, short and simple, and provide tips on how to solve the problem.

There are various approaches to error handling in React apps; let's review them. As an example, we will look at a failed network request.

First, and simplest, is to store the error in the state of the component. Whenever we make a server request, we can surround it in a `try-catch` block and store the error in state or in initial props:

```
// pages/index.js
import React from "react";

const faultyPromise = (client) => new Promise((resolve, reject) => {
    setTimeout(() => {
        reject(new Error('Faulty ' + (client ? 'client' : 'server')));
    }, 500);
});

export default class Page extends React.Component {
```

```
    state = {
        loading: false,
        error: null,
        result: null
    };

    static async loadPosts(client) {
        return await faultyPromise(client);
    }

    static async getInitialProps() {
        try {
            return {result: await Page.loadPosts(false)};
        } catch (e) {
            return {error: e.message};
        }
    }

    retry = async () => {
        this.setState({result: null, error: null, loading: true});
        try {
            this.setState({loading: false, result: await
Page.loadPosts(true)});
        } catch (e) {
            this.setState({loading: false, error: e.message});
        }
    };

    getError() {
        return (this.state.error || this.props.error);
    }

    getResult() {
        return (this.state.result || this.props.result);
    }

    isLoading() {
        return this.state.loading;
    }

    render() {
        if (this.state.loading) return (<div>Loading...</div>);

        const error = this.getError();
        if (error) return (
            <div>
                Cannot load posts: "{error}"
                <br/>
```

```
                <button onClick={this.retry}>Retry</button>
            </div>
        );

        return (
            <pre>{JSON.stringify(this.getResult())}</pre>
        );
    }
}
```

Here, we reuse the `loadPosts` static method both in initial load and for retries. The captured errors are stored and displayed to users.

But what if we forgot to capture the error somewhere or, more likely, the error happened somewhere down the component tree and we have no explicit way to `try-catch` it?

Luckily, React apps have the native ability to set error boundaries; consider the following example:

```
// pages/boundary.js
import React from "react";

class FaultyComponent extends React.Component {
    componentWillMount() {
        // only synchronous errors will be captured
        throw new Error('FaultyComponent threw an error');
    }

    render() {
        return null;
    }
}

export default class Page extends React.Component {

    state = {error: null, mount: false};

    componentDidCatch(e, info) {
        console.error(e, info);
        this.setState({error: e.message});
    }

    mount() {
        this.setState({mount: true});
    }

    render() {
```

```
        const {error, mount} = this.state;

        if (error) return (
            <div>Boundary captured an error: {error}</div>
        );

        return (
            <div>
                <button onClick={() => this.mount()}>Mount a component that
will error</button>
                {mount ? <FaultyComponent/> : null}
            </div>
        );
    }
}
```

Here, if the user clicks to mount the component, the error caused by `componentWillMount` will be captured by the page component and rendered. Keep in mind that errors cannot be captured on the server; you will see the Next.js error page. On the client, only synchronous errors will be captured; async ones will result in an unhandled rejection.

But what if we forgot the error boundary, or if something extremely horrible has happened, or the user has hit 404?

Let's emulate something like this:

```
// pages/unhandledError.js
import React from "react";

export default class UnhandledErrorPage extends React.Component {

    static async getInitialProps() {
        throw new Error('Unhandled error');
    }

    render() {
        return (
            <div>this will never appear in this example</div>
        );
    }
}
```

In this case, the user will see the Next.js error page:

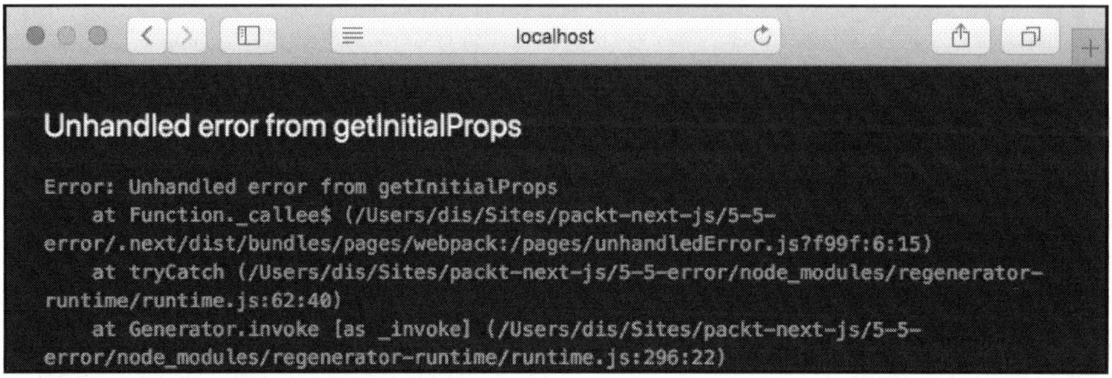

localhost

Unhandled error from getInitialProps

```
Error: Unhandled error from getInitialProps
    at Function._callee$ (/Users/dis/Sites/packt-next-js/5-5-error/.next/dist/bundles/pages/webpack:/pages/unhandledError.js?f99f:6:15)
    at tryCatch (/Users/dis/Sites/packt-next-js/5-5-error/node_modules/regenerator-runtime/runtime.js:62:40)
    at Generator.invoke [as _invoke] (/Users/dis/Sites/packt-next-js/5-5-error/node_modules/regenerator-runtime/runtime.js:296:22)
```

For 404s in Next.js, we can set up a special page:

```
// pages/_error.js
import React from 'react';
import Error from 'next/error';

export default class ErrorPage extends React.Component {

    componentWillMount() {
        // here we can log an error for further analysis, this will appear
in server's console
        console.log('NextJS Error Page', this.props.url.pathname);
    }

    render() {
        return (
            <Error statusCode={this.props.statusCode}/>
        );
    }
}
```

If the user visits `http://localhost:3000/thispageismissing`, they will see this:

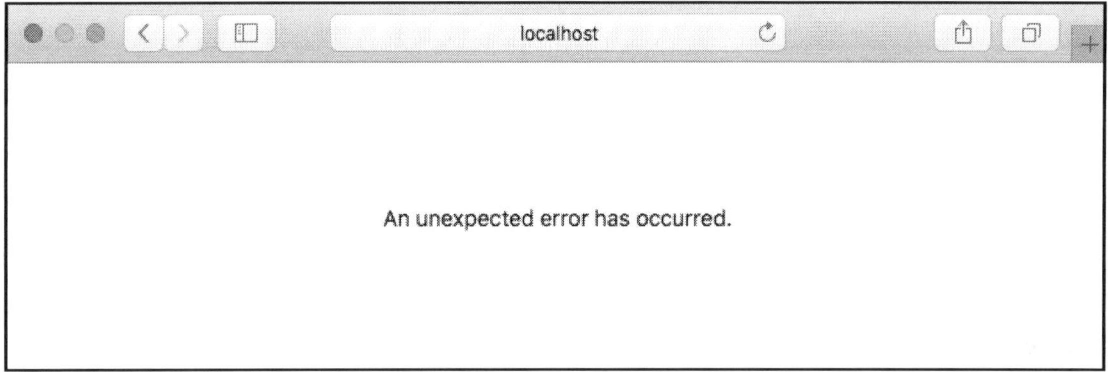

And in the console, there will be a message:

```
Client pings, but there's no entry for page: /thispageismissing
Unhandled error /thispageismissing
```

Caching

Caching could significantly improve the performance of the server because it will not try to request data from slow remote servers, but instead will access a fast local cache that can respond immediately.

We suggest using Redux on the client side because this will allow us to use `Store` as a runtime cache while the app is running. This approach also allows us to prepopulate some keys on the server when pages are loaded.

We recommend using client-side persistent storage for Redux extremely carefully, because improper usage may lead to state inconsistency between server and client: the server has sent some initial state, and the client then applies the extra initial state from localStorage (for example) and renders more than the server did, so you will get an error.

The client has to be smart enough to show the partial state from the server and then apply the delta coming from the persistor, without blocking the entire UI (like the `PersistGate` approach from `redux-persist`), because this ruins the overall idea of server-side rendering and the prepopulation of state.

After all, it is up to you to decide which way to go, so we will show both examples: when the client waits for state to be rehydrated and when it does not.

Let's install all packages, as always:

```
$ npm install next --save-dev
$ npm install react react-dom redux redux-logger react-redux next-redux-
wrapper redux-persist prop-types --save
```

Now, let's create the Redux setup:

```
// lib/redux.js
import logger from 'redux-logger';
import {applyMiddleware, createStore} from 'redux';

const SET_CLIENT_STATE = 'SET_CLIENT_STATE';

export const reducer = (state, {type, payload}) => {
    if (type == SET_CLIENT_STATE) {
        return {
            ...state,
            fromClient: payload
        };
    }
    return state;
};

const makeConfiguredStore = (reducer, initialState) =>
    createStore(reducer, initialState, applyMiddleware(logger));

export const makeStore = (initialState, {isServer, req, debug, storeKey})
=> {

    if (isServer) {

        // only do it now bc on client it should be undefined by default
        // server will put things in req
        initialState = initialState || {fromServer: 'foo'};

        return makeConfiguredStore(reducer, initialState);

    } else {

        const {persistStore, persistReducer} = require('redux-persist');
        const storage = require('redux-persist/lib/storage').default;

        const persistConfig = {
            key: 'nextjs',
            whitelist: ['fromClient'], // make sure it does not clash with
server keys
            storage
```

```
        };

        const persistedReducer = persistReducer(persistConfig, reducer);
        const store = makeConfiguredStore(persistedReducer, initialState);

        store.__persistor = persistStore(store); // Nasty hack

        return store;
    }
};

export const setClientState = (clientState) => ({
    type: SET_CLIENT_STATE,
    payload: clientState
});
```

Here, we exploit the possibility to inject a `persistor` right in the `store` object, so that we can later use it for `PersistGate`.

And now, we create the HOC to block the UI:

```
// lib/withPersistGate.js
import React from 'react';
import PropTypes from 'prop-types';
import {PersistGate} from 'redux-persist/integration/react';

export default (gateProps = {}) => (WrappedComponent) => (

    class WithPersistGate extends React.Component {

        static displayName =
`withPersistGate(${WrappedComponent.displayName
                                                  || WrappedComponent.name
                                                  || 'Component'})`;

        static contextTypes = {
            store: PropTypes.object.isRequired
        };

        constructor(props, context) {
            super(props, context);
            this.store = context.store;
        }

        render() {
            return (
                <PersistGate {...gateProps}
persistor={this.store.__persistor}>
                    <WrappedComponent {...this.props} />
```

```
                </PersistGate>
            );
        }

    }

);
```

Now, we can use it on the page:

```
// pages/index.js
import React from "react";
import Link from "next/link";
import withRedux from "next-redux-wrapper";
import {makeStore, setClientState} from "../lib/redux";
import withPersistGate from "../lib/withPersistGate";

const Index = ({fromServer, fromClient, setClientState}) => (
    <div>
        <div>fromServer: {fromServer}</div>
        <div>fromClient: {fromClient}</div>
        <div>
            <button onClick={e => setClientState('bar')}>Set Client
State</button>
        </div>
    </div>
);

export default withRedux(
    makeStore,
    (state) => state,
    {setClientState}
)(withPersistGate({
    loading: (<div>Loading</div>)
})(Index));
```

If you remove `withPersistGate`, the page will load part by part. As mentioned before, it's better to progressively render when the data comes instead of blocking, but for some cases, like when sub-components rely on the presence of certain data in the store in order to be displayed, it makes sense to put in the gate.

Analytics

No big project can live without gathering analytical information about their users, their habits and sources, and so on. A world leader in this field is Google Analytics, so let's create a simple integration between Next.js and this great product.

First, you need to create a project in Google Analytics and copy the ID:

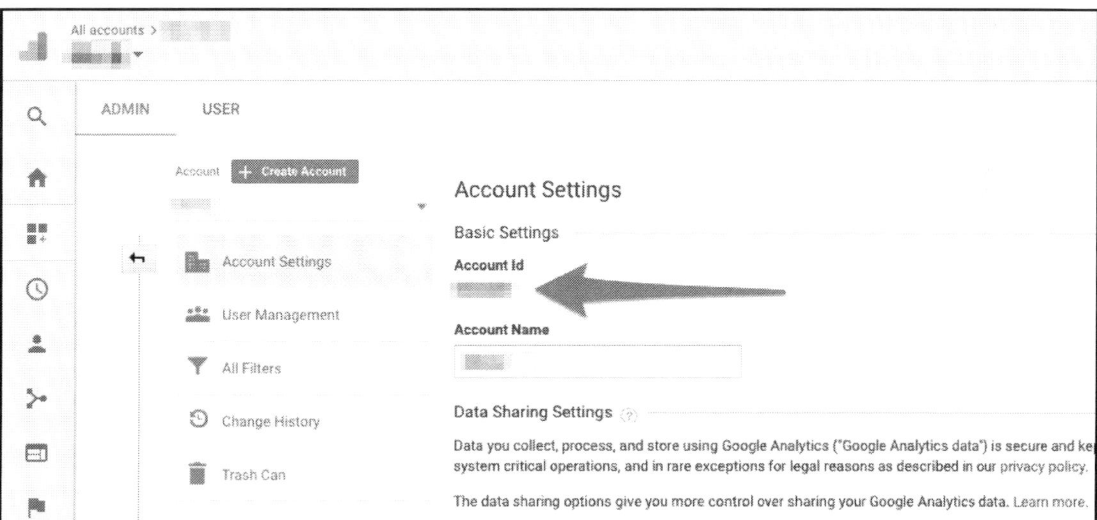

We start with packages:

```
$ npm install next --save-dev
$ npm install react react-dom react-ga --save
```

Next, let's create a HOC for pages that require analytics:

```
import React from "react";
import Router from 'next/router';
import ReactGA from 'react-ga';

const GA_TRACKING_ID = '...'; // paste your ID here
const WINDOWPROP = '__NEXT_GA_INITIALIZED__';
const debug = process.env.NODE_ENV !== 'production';

export default (WrappedComponent) => (class WithGA extends React.Component
{

    lastPath = null;
```

```
        componentDidMount() {
            this.initGa();
            this.trackPageview();
            Router.router.events.on('routeChangeComplete', this.trackPageview);
        }

        componentWillUnmount() {
            Router.router.events.off('routeChangeComplete',
    this.trackPageview);
        }

        trackPageview = (path = document.location.pathname) => {
            if (path === this.lastPath) return;
            ReactGA.pageview(path);
            this.lastPath = path;
        };

        initGa = () => {
            if (WINDOWPROP in window) return;
            ReactGA.initialize(GA_TRACKING_ID, {debug});
            window[WINDOWPROP] = true;
        };

        render() {
            return (
                <WrappedComponent {...this.props} />
            );
        }

    });
```

Here, we use some undocumented abilities of Next.js Router to capture location change events. It is not guaranteed that this API will be available in future; it just demonstrates the possibilities. Credits to `https://github.com/osartun`.

Now, let's wrap the page with the HOC:

```
import React from "react";
import withGA from "../lib/withGA";

const Index = () => (
    <div>Analyze this!</div>
);

export default withGA()(Index);
```

And this is it, all page views will be carefully logged.

Summary

In this chapter, we have learned some advanced patterns and how to implement and integrate them with Next.js. Let's recap what we have learned:

- Authentication
- Caching
- Internationalization
- Role-based access control
- Business rule management
- Error handling
- Analytics

Now, since our application is gaining more and more features, we can focus more on app integration and deployment. In the next chapter, we will cover this.

6
Continuous Integration

In previous chapters, we were learning how to write an application, but the application life cycle is not limited to just creating it. That is just the beginning of the journey. The app must survive all the upcoming updates and changes, and there has to be a set of tools and procedures that will guarantee it is still working properly. These tools and procedures have to provide measurable metrics to understand that things are doing OK.

In this chapter, we explain how to prepare the app for automatic deployment, and why unit and end-to-end tests are an important prerequisite for this. You will learn how to write tests and use online CI tools with Next.js.

In this chapter, we are going to cover the following topics:

- What is automated deployment?
- Writing unit tests for Next.js apps
- Writing end-to-end tests for Next.js apps
- Setting up CI for Next.js: Travis, Gitlab, and many more

What is automated deployment?

So far, most of the time we have only been dealing with the development mode of Next.js. But real-life projects have to be deployed on production servers at some point. And, of course, no sane person wants to deploy a product that has issues that will affect customers. After all, the main purpose of a product is to make customers happier. In order to make sure the quality of the product meets certain standards, the bare minimum is manual testing. This is when you or your QA colleague simply use the product and try to find all possible issues. Unfortunately, this is very time consuming and very ineffective as the project grows larger. Moreover, it is absolutely not guaranteed that any change in the system will not affect other parts of the system, so the only way to ensure quality is to test the entire system on every single change, which is completely impractical.

The problem becomes even bigger if the team grows too. The product will likely become very unstable and very unpredictable, even if each developer is very careful and tries to minimize the impact of each change. Unfortunately, sometimes we have to refactor large pieces and we definitely need some way to make sure we don't break anything.

Another factor is the turnaround speed. Imagine QA has found a bug in production; the bug was reported to you, the developer; you have fixed it locally; then you have to verify on your machine; then you need to put the build on the staging server (if there is one); verify there; then QA verifies; then you push the build to production and verify once again. Imagine how much time and manual labor this takes. And now, imagine that the fix was incorrect and in the production environment it still does not work. Now, you have to go through the same routine again without any confidence that your next fix will *actually* fix the problem.

In order to gain confidence that the product works well and not waste QA resources on endless retesting, the industry has come up with a number of best practices. So far, we have identified a few bottlenecks:

- Manual testing takes time
- Manual deployment takes time
- Uncertainty about the status of the system
- Uncertainty that the local fix works on production, that is, dev and prod environments are different

Manual testing can be partially replaced with unit and integration (end-to-end) tests; basically, we will automate what QA engineers do, and do it a thousand times quicker and much more reliably. Manual deployment can be automated by using deployment tools, which will auto-package and auto-upload where needed. Uncertainty about status can be mitigated by using code coverage and other kinds of reports; when tests are automated, it opens a way to gather statistics. The difference in environments can be fixed by using containers, a special way to reproduce 100% identical environments on different host machines.

All of this gives us the ability to automatically run unit and end-to-end tests on a dev machine in an environment that matches production; quickly fix issues locally, if there are any; then push changes to source control, where it will be picked up by the continuous integration server, which will re-run all tests to make sure everything works and then push the verified build to staging, where it can be quickly verified by manual QA. If it passes, the same build can be deployed to production, where, with a reasonable degree of confidence, it will most likely work as expected (sarcasm). This whole process is called continuous integration with automatic deployment.

Let's now review all of these methods.

Writing unit tests for Next.js apps

A unit test is a software testing method when modules and other granular parts of source code are tested independently in order to determine the correctness of their implementation. The key point of unit tests is that they should be small, cheap to run, and isolated. And there could be a ton of them to provide good coverage.

Writing unit tests for JavaScript nowadays is easier than ever before. With modern tools, the setup takes a few minutes and you can start getting the benefits right away. This includes coverage out of the box.

For this example, we will be using Jest and Enzyme – one of the most widespread frameworks for testing React apps. Jest provides a test runner and assertion engine, and Enzyme is used as a DOM manipulation/verification/traversal tool.

Let's install everything:

```
$ npm install react react-dom isomorphic-unfetch --save
$ npm install jest enzyme enzyme-adapter-react-16 next react-test-renderer
```

Now, we will configure Babel (which comes with both Next and Jest) to properly use the Next.js preset:

```
// .babelrc
{
  "env": {
    "test": {
      "presets": [
        [
          "env",
          {
            "modules": "commonjs"
          }
        ],
        "next/babel"
      ]
    },
    "development": {
      "presets": [
        "next/babel"
      ]
    }
  }
```

```
}
```

Here, we set babel-env-preset to use commonjs module notation and add the Next.js preset to both default and test environments.

Now, let's add the scripts section of package.json:

```
// package.json
{
  "scripts": {
    "start": "next",
    "test": "NODE_ENV=test jest"
  }
}
```

The next step will be to configure Jest:

```
// jest.config.js
module.exports = {
    setupFiles: [
        "./jest.setup.js"
    ],
    testPathIgnorePatterns: [
        "./.idea",
        "./.next",
        "./node_modules"
    ]
};
```

Here, we have configured the setup files that will be used to properly set up the test runtime and all the path patterns. It is important to exclude unnecessary directories from scans for test files and from coverage; this makes sure the test runs quickly and coverage is not bloated with extra files that we don't care about.

The next step would be to configure Enzyme; it is a framework that helps to test and verify React components:

```
// jest.setup.js
import {configure} from 'enzyme';
import Adapter from 'enzyme-adapter-react-16';

configure({adapter: new Adapter()});
```

Now, let's write tests! But... before we can do this we need some components, since we are not doing Test-Driven Development at the moment:

```
// lib/index.js
import 'isomorphic-unfetch';

export const sum = (a, b) => (a + b);

export const getOctocat = async () =>
    (await fetch('https://api.github.com/users/octocat')).json();
```

OK, now is the time to write the first test:

```
// lib/index.test.js
import {getOctocat, sum} from "./index";

describe('sum', () => {

    it('sums two values', () => {
        expect(sum(2, 2)).toEqual(4);
    });

});

describe('getOctocat', () => {

    it('fetches octocat userinfo from GitHub', async () => {
        const userinfo = await getOctocat();
        expect(userinfo.login).toEqual('octocat');
    });

});
```

Note the name of the file. There are many approaches to naming tests, but I prefer to put them next to the module with a `.test` suffix in the filename. Some people like to create a `__tests__`directory and put test files there. To me, the adjacent approach is more convenient when you scan through your repository, but that's just personal preference; Jest does not care, it will find tests anyway if files are named correctly.

The way tests work is very simple. We `describe` groups of tests defined in `it` functions (BDD style); inside those definitions, we make certain assertions by using `expect` functions. We can return a `Promise` if we want to do an async test, and async/await is also supported.

Now, let's create a sample page:

```
// pages/index.js
import React from "react";
import {getOctocat} from "../lib";

export default class Index extends React.Component {

    static async getInitialProps({err, req, res, pathname, query, asPath})
{
        const userinfo = await getOctocat();
        return {
            userinfo: userinfo
        };
    }

    render() {
        return (
            <div>Hello, {this.props.userinfo.login}!</div>
        );
    }

}
```

And here is a test for it:

```
// pages/index.test.js
import {shallow} from 'enzyme';
import React from 'react';
import renderer from 'react-test-renderer';
import Index from './index.js'

describe('Enzyme', () => {

    it('Renders "Hello octocat!" for given props', () => {
        const app = shallow(<Index userinfo={{login: 'octocat'}}/>);
        expect(app.find('div').text()).toEqual('Hello, octocat!');
    });

});

describe('Snapshot Testing', () => {

    it('Renders "Hello octocat!" for given props', () => {
        const component = renderer.create(<Index userinfo={{login:
'octocat'}}/>);
        const tree = component.toJSON();
        expect(tree).toMatchSnapshot();
```

```
    });

    it('Renders "Hello octocat!" for emulated NextJS lifecycle', async ()
=> {
        const userinfo = Index.getInitialProps({});
        const component = renderer.create(<Index userinfo={userinfo}/>);
        const tree = component.toJSON();
        expect(tree).toMatchSnapshot();
    });

});
```

Here, we have introduced two different approaches to testing React components:

- Classic assertion-based approach
- Snapshot testing

The first approach is the classic assertion-based approach just like in the previous library module: we create a rendered version of the component, grab its parts, and make assertions.

This approach is useful if we heavily work on the appearance of the component, rearrange things, alter the markup, and so on. Selectors should be concrete enough to find proper nodes, but at the same time relaxed enough to be less likely to break during the refactoring of the component. An ideal balance is attaching data attributes to leaf nodes like so:

```
<div className="wrapper">
    <div className="subwrapper">
        <h1 data-test-id="title">Foo</h1>
    </div>
</div>
```

In this case, a selector like `div.wrapper > div.subwrapper > h1` is way too strict and will break on every change. On the other hand, `h1` is too broad and if we have more than one `h1` in the component, the test will also become too fragile. Data attribute is an ideal balance between reachability and fragility of selector, so it's suggested to have something like this: `*[data-test-id=title]`.

The second approach is called snapshot testing. Instead of having to precisely take things from the renderer and make verbose assertions, we can render a snapshot and compare against it. The first time, this kind of test will surely pass, because there is nothing to compare with, so it's an instant success. Then, we can analyze the snapshot to see whether it's actually OK; we do this manually. The good snapshot can now be committed to the repository. Then, if anything changes in the component code, we will get an error that the snapshot does not match the current outcome. At this point, we will have some options: if the mismatch is intended and after analysis we confirm that everything is right, we can update the snapshot and commit it; or, if we determined that something is wrong and the resulting HTML does not satisfy the requirement, we can fix this.

This approach is suitable for things that rarely change their appearance, but where underlying code is being refactored.

Also, we have tested the emulated Next.js behavior by manually calling `getInitialProps` and injecting the result into the component.

After this, we run the test using:

```
$ npm test
```

If you need to update test snapshots, you may do it like so:

```
$ npm test -- --updateSnapshot                              # this updates all
$ npm test -- --updateSnapshot --testNamePattern foo   # this updates
specific test
```

Writing end-to-end tests for Next.js apps

The emulated test that we made in the previous chapter is OK, but what if we would like to make a full fledged test to verify that everything is good from the end user's perspective? Such tests are called integration tests or **end-to-end** (**e2e**) tests.

Unlike unit tests, where we test everything in maximum isolation, module by module, with stubs for external services and so on, this kind of test covers as many modules at once as possible, to make sure all of them work together properly, including integration with third parties. Basically, such a test emulates regular user behavior. The main aim is to make sure that user scenarios work well and all the involved business logic is correct.

This is a very expensive kind of test. Different companies have different policies regarding the coverage of unit vs e2e tests. Normally, unit test coverage should be above 90%, and e2e should be around at least 20-30%, but the quality of this coverage has to be very high, for example, it should test the scenarios with the highest business value, such as signup or purchasing something.

The purpose of the test suggests that we should use a real browser to run the test. This way, we can emulate a user as closely as possible, meaning that it would be real clicks and real inputs.

We will use the simple solution with a headless Chromium browser. However, when your project grows large enough, you may use something much more sophisticated such as a Selenium Grid. We will use Jest Puppeteer, a package that provides a glue layer between these two frameworks.

Let's install the packages:

```
$ npm install react react-dom isomorphic-unfetch --save
$ npm install jest jest-puppeteer puppeteer next --save-dev
```

As usual, we should put the `start` and `test` scripts in `package.json`:

```
// package.json
{
  "scripts": {
    "start": "next",
    "test": "NODE_ENV=test jest"
  }
}
```

Now, let's configure Jest and Jest Puppeteer:

```
// jest.config.js
module.exports = {
    preset: 'jest-puppeteer',
    testPathIgnorePatterns: [
        './.idea',
        './.next',
        './node_modules'
    ]
};
```

We're using a special preset that takes care of the Puppeteer setup for Jest:

```
// jest-puppeteer.js
module.exports = {
    server: {
        command: 'npm start',
        port: 3000,
        launchTimeout: 30000
    }
};
```

We have instructed the glue layer to launch our development server before we run the tests.

Now, let's create a page:

```
// pages/index.js
import 'isomorphic-unfetch';
import React from "react";

export default class Index extends React.Component {

    static async getInitialProps({err, req, res, pathname, query, asPath})
{
        const userinfo = await (await
fetch('https://api.github.com/users/octocat')).json();
        return {
            userinfo: userinfo
        };
    }

    state = {
        clicked: false
    };

    handleClick = (e) => {
        this.setState({clicked: true});
    };

    render() {
        return (
            <div className="index">
                <div>Hello, {this.props.userinfo.login}!</div>
                <div>
                    <button onClick={this.handleClick}>Click</button>
                </div>
                {this.state.clicked && (<div>Clicked</div>)}
            </div>
```

```
        );
    }

}
```

We have created a simple page that loads a user from GitHub and displays it. Also, it shows a clickable button; when clicked, text appears next to the button. Notice the `class="index"` on the root `div`; we will use it to determine that the page is rendered.

Finally, let's write a test:

```
const config = require('../jest-puppeteer.config');

const openPage = (url = '/') =>
page.goto(`http://localhost:${config.server.port}${url}`);

describe('Basic integration', () => {

    it('shows the page', async () => {
        await openPage();
        await page.waitForSelector('div.index'); // wait for page to be
rendered
        // we will simply check all text of the page instead of individual
checks
        await expect(page).toMatch('Hello, octocat!Click');
    });

    it('clicks the button', async () => {
        await openPage();
        await page.waitForSelector('div.index'); // wait for page to be
rendered
        await expect(page).toClick('button', {text: 'Click'});
        // we will simply check all text of the page instead of individual
checks
        await expect(page).toMatch('Hello, octocat!ClickClicked');
    });

});
```

Here, we have two tests: one simply checks that the page exists and shows the correct text, and the second one tests that the button is clickable and the reaction on click is right. We used an additional API of `expect-puppeteer` to conveniently write assertions. Also, we used `await page.waitForSelector('div.index');` to make sure that Next.js has built everything and the page is properly rendered. Otherwise, Jest and Puppeteer will not know when the Next.js dev build will be ready and when the page will finally be rendered.

You can read more about this integration and API here: https://github.com/smooth-code/jest-puppeteer#writing-tests-using-puppeteer.

Setting up CI for Next.js: Travis, Gitlab, and so on

Running tests on a local dev machine is fun, but things happen. You may forget to run a test before commit (in the next chapter, you will learn how to prevent this), or any of your team members can accidentally break something. In order to make sure everything works, you need some centralized source of truth. This source of truth could be a TravisCI server, which is free for open source projects. For private projects, there is another free solution, which we will cover too.

First, register or log in to http://travis-ci.org:

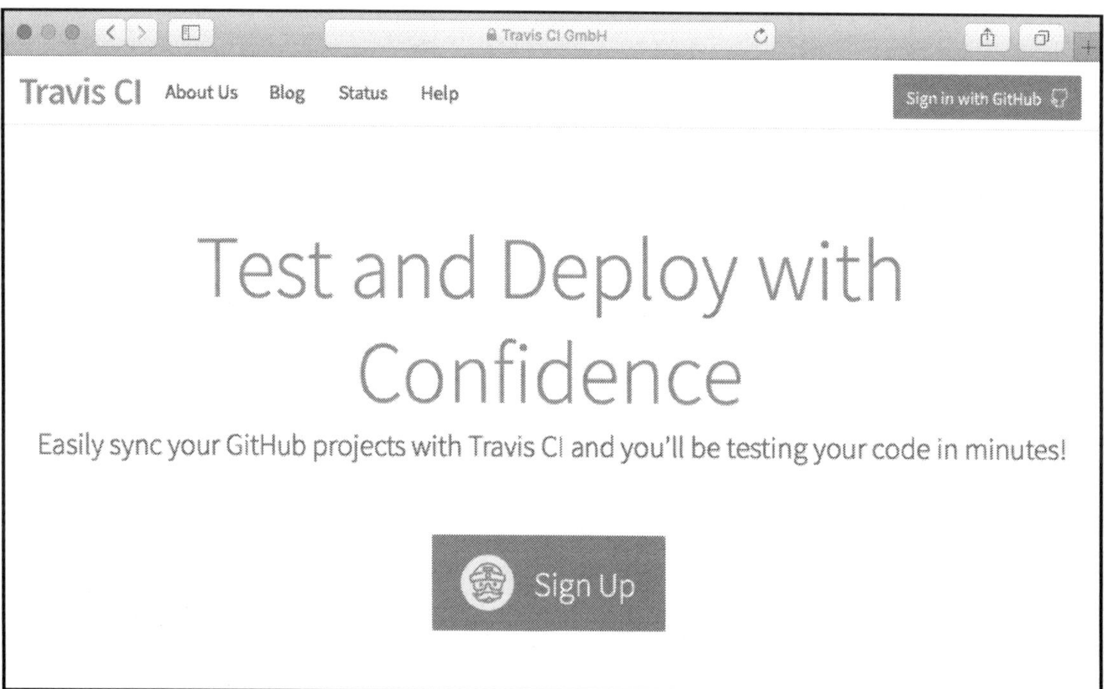

You will have to enter your GitHub credentials in order to proceed, then once you have logged in, go to your profile page and flick the switch next to your repository:

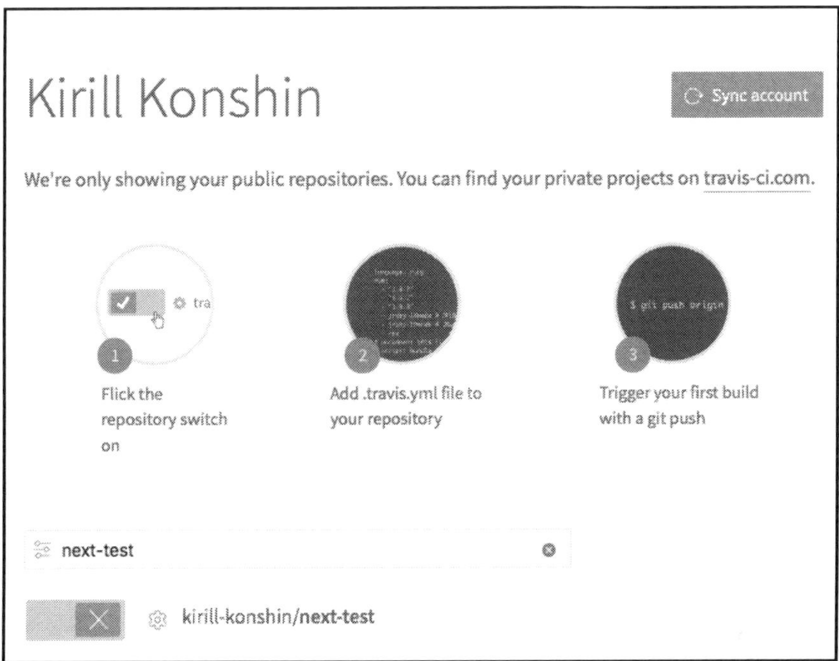

If there are no repositories, just click **Sync Account** to reload them.

You may want to set up some environment variables for the build; it is good practice to securely store all credentials there.

The most minimalistic setup for TravisCI will be the following (in the `.travis.yml` file):

```
language: node_js
node_js:
- stable
```

TravisCI knows that you're using a Node.js setup so it will automatically do `npm install` and then `npm test` for you. If you need to perform anything additional, you may add more scripts before or after the test run; we will show an example later.

You can now either push a commit to GitHub, which will trigger TravisCI build and test run, or you can go to your GitHub repository at **Settings** | **Integrations & Services**, find **Travis CI**, and click **Edit** | **Test Service** at the top of the main panel.

As a result of the build, you will see the following in the console (assuming you've run the example from `Chapter 5`, *Application Life Cycle Handlers and Business Logic*):

```
Raw log
mode of '/usr/local/clang-5.0.0/bin' changed from 0777 (rwxrwxrwx) to 0775 (rwxrwxr-x)
Build system information

removed '/etc/apt/sources.list.d/basho_riak.list'
Network availability confirmed.
127.0.0.1       localhost
::1      ip6-localhost ip6-loopback
fe00::0 ip6-localnet
ff00::0 ip6-mcastprefix
ff02::1 ip6-allnodes
ff02::2 ip6-allrouters
172.17.0.9      travis-job-kirill-konshin-next-test-367426849.travisci.net travis-job-kirill-konshin-next-test-
367426849
W: http://ppa.launchpad.net/couchdb/stable/ubuntu/dists/trusty/Release.gpg: Signature by key
15866BAFD9BCC4F3C1E0DFC7D69548E1C17EAB57 uses weak digest algorithm (SHA1)
$ git clone --depth=50 --branch=master https://github.com/kirill-konshin/next-test.git
$ export PATH=./node_modules/.bin:$PATH
Updating nvm
$ nvm install stable
$ node --version
v9.11.1
$ npm --version
5.6.0
$ nvm --version
0.33.8
$ npm install
$ npm test

> 6-3-e2e-tests@1.0.0 test /home/travis/build/kirill-konshin/next-test
> NODE_ENV=test jest

 PASS  pages/index.test.js
  Basic integration
    ✓ shows the page (2597ms)
    ✓ clicks the button (305ms)

Test Suites: 1 passed, 1 total
Tests:       2 passed, 2 total
Snapshots:   0 total
Time:        4.11s
Ran all test suites.
Killed


The command "npm test" exited with 0.

Done. Your build exited with 0.
Top
```

Now, let's take a look at another CI solution: **GitLab**.

Once you've registered, created a repository, and uploaded your code there, create a file called `.gitlab-ci.yml`:

```
image: node:latest

cache:
  paths:
  - node_modules/

test:
  script:
  - apt-get update
  - apt-get install -yq gconf-service libasound2 libatk1.0-0 libc6
libcairo2 libcups2 libdbus-1-3 libexpat1 libfontconfig1 libgcc1
libgconf-2-4 libgdk-pixbuf2.0-0 libglib2.0-0 libgtk-3-0 libnspr4
libpango-1.0-0 libpangocairo-1.0-0 libstdc++6 libx11-6 libx11-xcb1 libxcb1
libxcomposite1 libxcursor1 libxdamage1 libxext6 libxfixes3 libxi6
libxrandr2 libxrender1 libxss1 libxtst6 ca-certificates fonts-liberation
libappindicator1 libnss3 lsb-release xdg-utils wget
  - npm install
  - npm test
```

This super-long list of dependencies shows requirements for Puppeteer to launch Chrome in Docker.

Then, after committing, you may go to **CI/CD** | **Pipelines** and click on the pipeline to see the following console output:

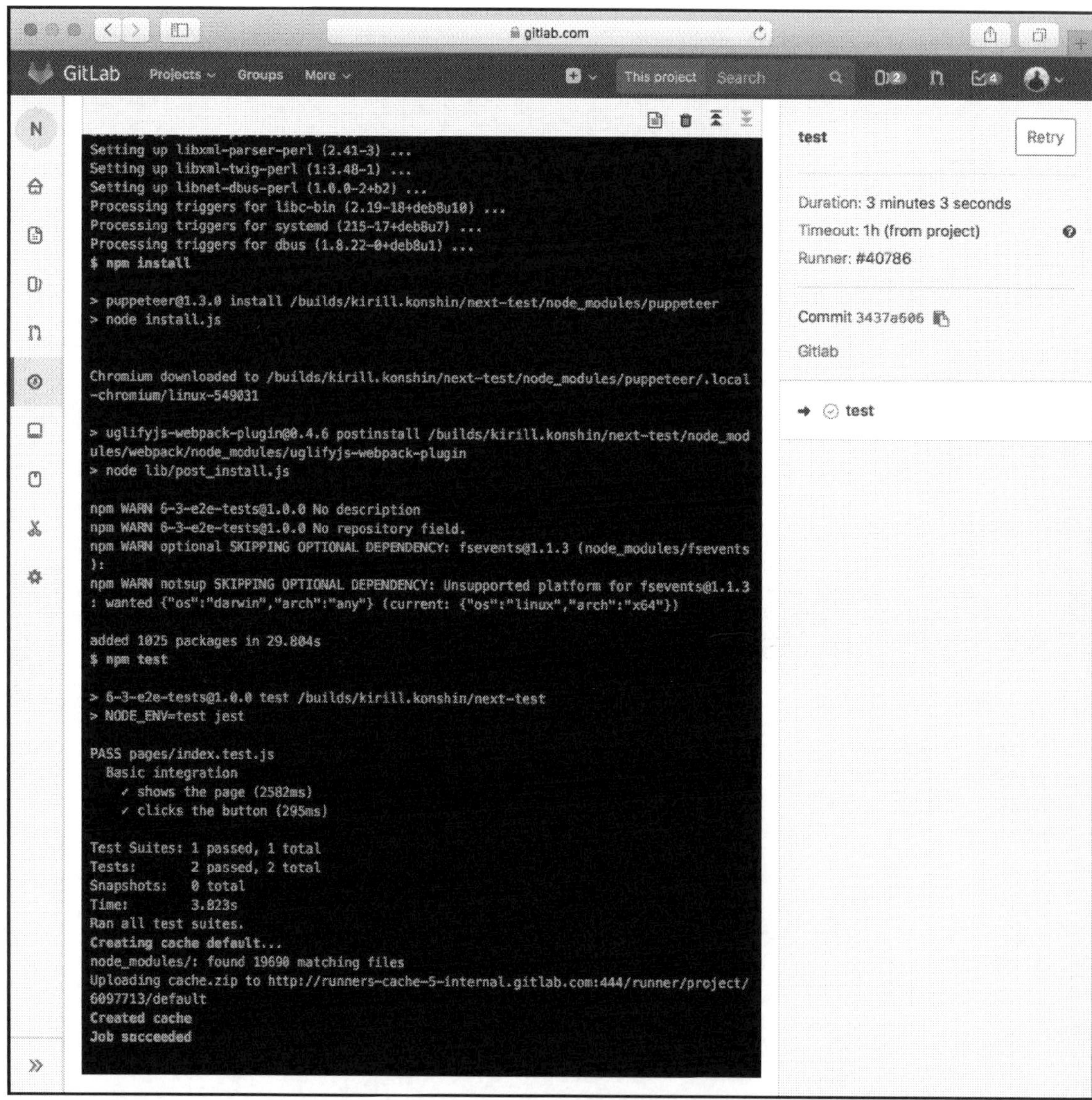

Keep in mind that it is better to keep your e2e test files separate from the code base, so that you won't accidentally import anything from there. Do not mix the contexts.

Setting up cloud coverage statistics

It is very useful to track coverage status changes after commits:

- It reveals risky changes early
- It gives a clear warning to go ahead and fix it before it gets out of hand

For this example, we will use a free service called Coveralls:

```
$ npm install react react-dom --save
$ npm install coveralls jest next react-test-renderer --save-dev
```

Same as before; we need to configure Babel too:

```
// .babelrc
{
  "env": {
    "test": {
      "presets": [
        [
          "env",
          {
            "modules": "commonjs"
          }
        ],
        "next/babel"
      ]
    },
    "development": {
      "presets": [
        "next/babel"
      ]
    }
  }
}
```

Let's configure Jest to collect coverage for us:

```
// jest.config.js
module.exports = {
    testPathIgnorePatterns: [
        './.idea',
        './.next',
        './node_modules'
    ],
    collectCoverage: true,
    coverageDirectory: './coverage',
```

```
        coveragePathIgnorePatterns: [
            "./node_modules"
            // also exclude your setup files here if you have any
        ]
    };
```

We will get a coverage report both in the console and in the `coverage` folder.

Now, let's add a script to `package.json`:

```
// package.json
{
  "scripts": {
    "test": "NODE_ENV=test jest",
    "coveralls": "cat ./coverage/lcov.info | coveralls",
  }
}
```

This will pipe the output from the Jest coverage reporter to the Coveralls executable, which will upload it to the cloud.

In order to call this script, we should update the `.travis.yml` file (or any other CI config that you have chosen):

```
# .travis.yml
language: node_js
node_js:
- stable
after_success:
- npm run coveralls
```

Or if you use GitLab, update `.gitlab-ci.yml`:

```
# .gitlab-ci.yml
image: node:latest

cache:
  paths:
  - node_modules/

test:
  script:
  - apt-get update
  - apt-get install -yq gconf-service libasound2 libatk1.0-0 libc6
libcairo2 libcups2 libdbus-1-3 libexpat1 libfontconfig1 libgcc1
libgconf-2-4 libgdk-pixbuf2.0-0 libglib2.0-0 libgtk-3-0 libnspr4
libpango-1.0-0 libpangocairo-1.0-0 libstdc++6 libx11-6 libx11-xcb1 libxcb1
libxcomposite1 libxcursor1 libxdamage1 libxext6 libxfixes3 libxi6
```

```
libxrandr2 libxrender1 libxss1 libxtst6 ca-certificates fonts-liberation
libappindicator1 libnss3 lsb-release xdg-utils wget
  - npm install
  - npm test
  - npm run coveralls
```

And this is it: commit, push, and see how coverage is being uploaded and stored by Coveralls.

Commit hooks

The most common reason for failed tests on CI is when a developer forgets to run the tests locally. Code in a repository can contain bugs, that's a given, but at least it should never have bugs that could be found by tests, so running tests before a commit is a mandatory practice in lots of companies.

Let's follow this best practice. We will use a library called Husky, which can wire to Git hooks to run desired scripts.

We start with packages, as always:

```
$ npm install husky --save-dev
```

Next, we need to set scripts in `package.json`:

```
// package.json
{
  "scripts": {
    "test": "NODE_ENV=test jest",
    "precommit": "npm test"
  }
}
```

And this is it; from now on, before any commit, Husky will run your tests. So, there will be fewer surprises after pushes.

Summary

In this chapter, we learned how to integrate the app into the deployment life cycle, and what test automation and continuous integration are. Now, when this important prerequisite is satisfied, we can deploy the app. In the next chapter, we will learn how to do just that.

7
Containers

In the previous chapter, we learned how to make sure the app still works if we make changes. But, this is still not the final step in the application life cycle. Once written and tested, the app has to be deployed somewhere to open it to the rest of the world. Deployment means that you create some sort of build artifact (something that appears after you run a build procedure) and place it on a computer that can take this artifact and reveal it to the internet. The simplest way is to zip all the build/out folder, upload it to a remote server, and extract it. But this is very inconvenient when an update contains deletions, edits, additions, and so on. Moreover, what if the server software has to also be updated during the deployment? There has to be a better way.

In this chapter, you will learn what virtual machine containers are and why they are useful. You will learn the most popular container framework, Docker, and how to configure an image for it. After that, you will learn how to deploy your application to online services that provide container-based infrastructure.

In this chapter, we will cover the following topics:

- What is a container for a Next.js app?
- Creating a Docker container for Next.js
- Deploying to Heroku and Now.sh

What is a container for a Next.js app?

In the previous chapter, we covered tests as a must-have prerequisite for automated deployment. Now, let's take a closer look at the other part: deployment and reproducibility of the production environment.

Modern virtualization technologies allow us to create cheap virtual machines; this is essentially an emulated computer running on a real computer, with an operating system, I/O, and everything else. From the viewpoint of a program that runs inside a VM, it is almost indistinguishable from the real computer, at least if the program does not touch low-level interfaces, which is highly unlikely if you do regular web development.

Since everything on a virtual machine is controlled by the host, memory, CPU, storage, everything, we can make snapshots of the virtual machine. Later, we can use those snapshots to transition the VM from one state to another. We even can write a script that will, step by step, bring a seed state to some final state, say, an empty Linux OS to a state with Node.js and other software installed. These states can be tagged and stored.

There are several technologies that allow us to do this, for example, Vagrant and Docker. The main difference is that Vagrant is a virtual machine manager, whereas Docker is a container manager. A container image is a lightweight, standalone, executable package of a piece of software that includes everything needed to run it: code, runtime, system tools, system libraries, and settings. The main difference is that a container is an operating system-level virtualization and Vagrant is a machine-level virtualization. Containers are much cheaper (in terms of resources and thus money) than VMs because they can run on one OS instance and don't have overheads of multiple completely isolated VMs, each with their own OS.

For our purposes, containers will work better primarily because they provide enough functionality to run isolated reproducible environments with minimum overhead.

Creating a Docker container for Next.js

Let's reiterate: Docker is a virtual machine with an OS that is capable of managing containers. So, how to bring the container image to a required tools, libs and settings? Via an instruction file, of course, because this process has to be reproducible on a dev machine, in staging, in production, and anywhere else.

A Dockerfile is a set of instructions that take a source image and bring it to a desired state, which results in an image too. Any existing Dockerfile's outcome image could in turn be taken as a source for another one, and so on.

Let's start with a super-minimal set of packages:

```
$ npm i react react-dom isomorphic-unfetch --save
$ npm i next --save-dev
```

Next, we create `scripts` in `package.json` as usual:

```
{
  "scripts": {
    "start": "next",
    "build": "next build",
    "server": "next server"
  }
}
```

Let's create our very first Docker file. We start with the official Node.js image, and each step will create an intermediate image:

```
FROM node:latest
```

This line says that we would like to take the latest Node.js image as the foundation.

```
WORKDIR /app
```

This is basically a CD inside a directory inside the container. It will be created if it does not exist.

```
ADD package.json .npmrc ./
```

We add `package.json` and `.npmrc` to the container; it's like a copy but to a different OS.

```
ENV NPM_CONFIG_LOGLEVEL warn
```

Set the environment variable, in this case, silence npm's verboseness.

```
RUN npm install
```

Here, we simply execute a command because the container system has only `package.json` and `.npmrc`, so until those two files change, Docker will cache the resulting container after `npm install`, which means if nothing changed, no installation will happen and an intermediate container will be taken from cache. This is the power of Docker: we can later change anything in our sources but the cached image with the installed modules will not be rebuilt until we touch the package.

```
ADD pages ./pages
```

Now, we copy the rest of the code base (adding more directories if needed).

```
RUN NODE_ENV=production npm run build
```

Then, since we have the sources, we can run the main build.

```
CMD NODE_ENV=production npm run server
```

And finally, we specify the command that will be used as the main long-running script.

Here is the resulting `Dockerfile`:

```
# Dockerfile
FROM node:latest
WORKDIR /app
ADD package.json .npmrc ./
ENV NPM_CONFIG_LOGLEVEL warn
RUN npm install
ADD pages ./pages
RUN NODE_ENV=production npm run build
CMD NODE_ENV=production npm run server
```

Now, we can build the image and tag it as `nextjs`:

```
$ docker build --tag nextjs .
```

This will produce something like this as console output:

```
$ docker build --tag nextjs .

Sending build context to Docker daemon 84.38MB
Step 1/8 : FROM node:latest
 ---> c1d02ac1d9b4
Step 2/8 : WORKDIR /app
 ---> Using cache
 ---> 7ad698557939
Step 3/8 : ADD package.json .npmrc ./
 ---> 62c7aedf5cb2
Step 4/8 : ENV NPM_CONFIG_LOGLEVEL warn
 ---> Running in e8164d671ffb
Removing intermediate container e8164d671ffb
 ---> 7aa21abc3f66
Step 5/8 : RUN npm install
 ---> Running in 4eef79cb0ac8
added 776 packages in 15.263s
Removing intermediate container 4eef79cb0ac8
 ---> a412d0bc3e0e
Step 6/8 : ADD pages ./pages
 ---> e51e7e209b37
Step 7/8 : RUN NODE_ENV=production npm run build
 ---> Running in 4848bec94bbd
> 7-2-docker-ssr@1.0.0 build /app
> next build
Removing intermediate container 4848bec94bbd
 ---> cbd50a380abb
Step 8/8 : CMD NODE_ENV=production npm run server
```

```
 ---> Running in bacd03b2fe05
Removing intermediate container bacd03b2fe05
 ---> 77a221cb892d
Successfully built 77a221cb892d
```

Now, let's run the container using the previously created `nextjs` tag:

```
$ docker run -p 8080:3000 nextjs
```

Here, we mapped local port `8080` to container port `3000` (the default port of Next.js) and ran the tagged container `nextjs`. The output will be like so:

```
> 7-2-docker-ssr@1.0.0 server /app
> next start
> Ready on http://localhost:3000
```

The message `Ready on http://localhost:3000` means CONTAINER port; in order to access the server from your browser, you must use LOCAL port, which is `8080`.

Basically, this can already be used in production.

But there is another method for using Next.js, a static build, and it requires another kind of setup.

Let's refresh ourselves on what a static build is. It is a version of a website that can be served statically from any web server, such as Apache or Nginx, which suggests that we will need both Node.js to build and Apache/Nginx to run. Of course, we can make one Dockerfile with both services, but it will be very wasteful in terms of space — Node.js is needed only to build, so if the resulting image will still contain it, it's wasted space as Node.js will not be present at runtime. Some time ago, we'd create two Dockerfiles, build and run them sequentially, and one would be a builder while the second one would be a server, but this is not very convenient. Luckily, in the latest versions of Docker, a technology called multi-stage build was introduced. It allows us to take files from one image and add them to another image.

Let's add a static build to `package.json` scripts first:

```
// package.json
{
  "scripts": {
    "static": "next export"
  }
}
```

Then, we have to add a `next.config.js` with a pathmap:

```
// next.config.js
module.exports = {
    exportPathMap: () => ({
        '/': {page: '/'}
    })
};
```

Now, let's create a `Dockerfile`; the first part will be the same as before:

```
# Dockerfile
FROM node:latest as build
WORKDIR /app
ADD package.json .npmrc ./
ENV NPM_CONFIG_LOGLEVEL warn
RUN npm install
ADD pages next.config.js ./
RUN NODE_ENV=production npm run build
RUN NODE_ENV=production npm run static
```

Notice that this file no longer has a CMD section because there is nothing to be executed as daemon; nothing will run at runtime.

Now, let's write the second part of the `Dockerfile`, which runs Nginx with a static build from the first part:

```
# Dockerfile
FROM nginx:latest AS production
RUN mkdir -p /usr/share/nginx/html
WORKDIR /usr/share/nginx/html
COPY --from=build /app/out .
```

Notice that we have copied files from the `build` container's (`--from=build`) directory, `/app/out`, to the current working directory of the `production` container.

Now, let's try it out:

```
$ docker build --tag nextjs .
$ docker run -p 8080:80 nextjs
```

Open your browser and open the page at `http://localhost:8080`, and you should see `Hello, octocat!` in the browser and the terminal output should look like this (some lines were omitted for compactness):

```
$ docker build --tag nextjs .

Sending build context to Docker daemon 60.95MB
Step 1/13 : FROM node:latest as build
latest: Pulling from library/node
Digest:
sha256:bd7b9aaf77ab2ce1e83e7e79fc0969229214f9126ced222c64eab49dc0bdae90
Status: Downloaded newer image for node:latest
 ---> aa3e171e4e95
Step 2/13 : WORKDIR /app
Removing intermediate container 16976f79c64b
 ---> f32ea6e77a9a
Step 3/13 : ADD package.json .npmrc ./
 ---> 072e1f684d0b
Step 4/13 : ENV NPM_CONFIG_LOGLEVEL warn
 ---> Running in c57d28703d1a
Removing intermediate container c57d28703d1a
 ---> f93784ce430f
Step 5/13 : RUN npm install
 ---> Running in 42d4a0a46e6a
added 660 packages in 14.655s
Removing intermediate container 42d4a0a46e6a
 ---> 9e0fe68685e5
Step 6/13 : ADD pages next.config.js ./
 ---> e4b68980279e
Step 8/13 : RUN NODE_ENV=production npm run build
 ---> Running in d4be23864c46
> 7-2-docker-static@1.0.0 build /app
> next build
Removing intermediate container d4be23864c46
 ---> b69fbf6dec0e
Step 9/13 : RUN NODE_ENV=production npm run static
 ---> Running in 7b946925c7c2
> 7-2-docker-static@1.0.0 static /app
> next export
  using build directory: /app/.next
  exporting path: /
Removing intermediate container 7b946925c7c2
 ---> 9e2b0fe9251a
Step 10/13 : FROM nginx:latest AS production
latest: Pulling from library/nginx
Digest:
sha256:18156dcd747677b03968621b2729d46021ce83a5bc15118e5bcced925fb4ebb9
Status: Downloaded newer image for nginx:latest
```

```
 ---> b175e7467d66
Step 11/13 : RUN mkdir -p /usr/share/nginx/html
 ---> Running in 568c1743f3de
Removing intermediate container 568c1743f3de
 ---> 36d271661cca
Step 12/13 : WORKDIR /usr/share/nginx/html
Removing intermediate container 2a199ef4bc5d
 ---> 00fe8c21e4be
Step 13/13 : COPY --from=build /app/out .
 ---> c9d050120ef9
Successfully built c9d050120ef9
Successfully tagged nextjs:latest

$ docker run -p 8080:80 nextjs

172.17.0.1 - - [17/Apr/2018:03:39:26 +0000] "GET / HTTP/1.1" 200 2560 "-"
... blah
172.17.0.1 - - [17/Apr/2018:03:39:26 +0000] "GET /_next/ ... blah
172.17.0.1 - - [17/Apr/2018:03:39:26 +0000] "GET /_next/ ... blah
172.17.0.1 - - [17/Apr/2018:03:39:26 +0000] "GET /_next/ ... blah
```

The resulting image is pure Nginx, with only a build and nothing else. We can make it even leaner by taking a different source image for the second phase, but that's out of scope for now.

Now, you can take the resulting image and upload it to your production Docker machine, but then you'll need a private repository or you should use Amazon's AWS or something similar, where you can upload images. Or, you can run the same commands (build and run) on your production machine, given it has access to your Git repository. Both approaches work, but the approach where you build in production is kind of awkward; build on builder machines or locally, and run production images on production machines. After all, production only takes care of images, it should not know how the image was created. Also, it is wasteful to build an image every time you deploy on a machine, especially if you have lots of machines for redundancy.

In order to do a complete CI, your server should be capable of building Docker images on successful test runs and deploying them automatically. This could be achieved with Gitlab, GitHub, and Travis, of course, but we are not covering this right now since there are simpler solutions.

Deploying to Heroku

Taking care of the health of your Node.js server in server-side rendering mode can be tricky; you have to monitor the different parameters, you have to take care of logs, and do all the other operational things. Nowadays, lots of providers offer free and paid servers, where you can deploy apps without the necessity of diving into server-side specifics; you write apps, and they do the rest.

A popular service called Heroku (`http://heroku.com`) offers various servers for different languages, including JS and Node.js in particular; they have optimized containers that can run your apps.

After you have signed up to **Heroku**, create a new project, name it, and once created, click **Connect to Github**. Type in the name of the repository and click **Connect**:

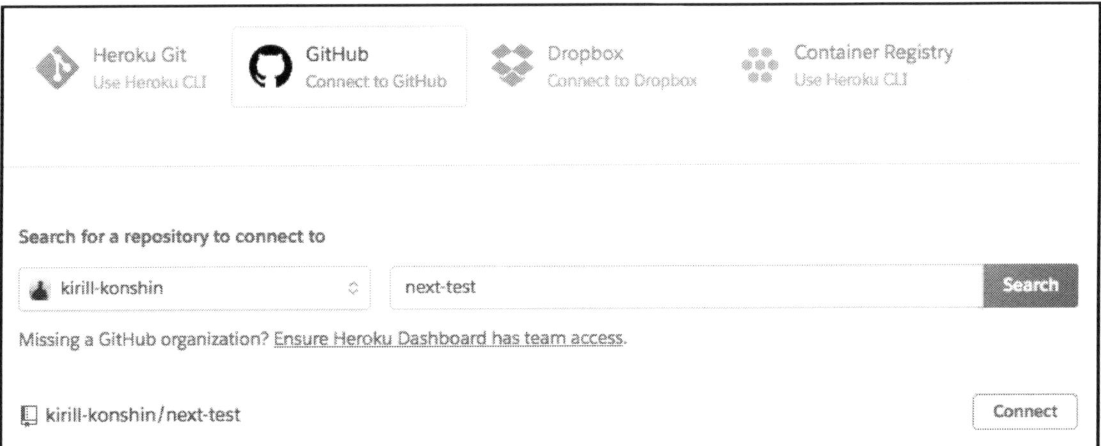

If you want everything to be fully automatic, click **Wait for CI to pass before deploy** (we assume you have already added Travis integration) and click **Enable Automatic Deploys**:

Automatic deploys
Enables a chosen branch to be automatically deployed to this app.
Enable automatic deploys from GitHub
Every push to the branch you specify here will deploy a new version of this app. **Deploys happen automatically:** be sure that this branch is always in a deployable state and any tests have passed before you push. Learn more.
master
Wait for CI to pass before deploy
Only enable this option if you have a Continuous Integration service configured on your repo.
Enable Automatic Deploys

Manual deploy
Deploy the current state of a branch to this app.
Deploy a GitHub branch
This will deploy the current state of the branch you specify below. Learn more.
master
Deploy Branch

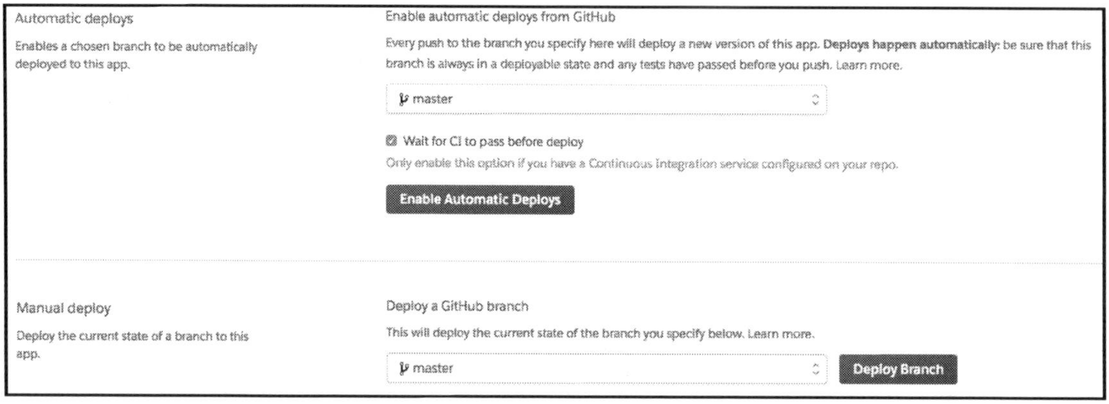

Now, let's configure our app to be Heroku-compatible. First, let's modify the scripts of `package.json`:

```
// package.json
{
  "scripts": {
    "heroku-postbuild": "next build",
    "start": "next",
    "server": "next start",
    "test": "NODE_ENV=test jest"
  }
}
```

Here, we have the following scripts: `start` for dev, `server` for production server, and `heroku-postbuild` in order to call the Next.js build for Heroku.

Next, we need to teach Heroku to run the proper command; for this, we create a `Procfile`:

```
web: npm run server -- --port $PORT
```

Here, we use a `-- whatever` syntax to pass parameters to the `npm script` (the same as we did before), Heroku opens an internal port (which could have any value) on the machine and proxies it to external ports, and it creates an `ENV` variable `PORT` with the port value, so we have to use this variable for our script to run on a proper port.

You can install the Heroku CLI and use the following command to verify that it will run the proper script:

```
$ heroku local web
```

Now, just commit all the new stuff and wait for CI to pass or hit the **Deploy branch** button if you're not patient. Once everything is done, you can open your app at `https://yourappname.herokuapp.com`. After the first run, which can take some time, you will see your app.

Deploying to Now.sh

Heroku is a well known workhorse, but nowadays there are newer players that can do things even easier, for example, `Now.sh`.

In addition to the previous example, just add one more `script` with the now-specific name `now-start` to `package.json`:

```
// package.json
{
  "scripts": {
    "heroku-postbuild": "npm run build",
    "build": "next build",
    "start": "next",
    "server": "next start",
    "now-start": "npm run server",
    "test": "NODE_ENV=test jest"
  }
}
```

Then, install Now Desktop from their website, register/login, and run this:

```
$ now
```

That will produce something like this:

```
$ now

> Your credentials and configuration were migrated to "~/.now"
> Deploying ~/Sites/next-test under xxx
> Your deployment's code and logs will be publicly accessible because you
are subscribed to the OSS plan.
> NOTE: You can use `now --public` or upgrade your plan
(https://zeit.co/account/plan) to skip this prompt
> Using Node.js 8.11.1 (default)
```

```
> https://xxx.now.sh [in clipboard] (sfo1) [4s]
> Synced 9 files (351.6KB) [4s]
> Building...
> ▲ npm install
> ✓ Using "package-lock.json"
>  Installing 7 main dependencies...
> ▲ npm run build
> 6-3-e2e-tests@1.0.0 build /home/nowuser/src
> next build
> ▲ Snapshotting deployment
> ▲ Saving deployment image (107.8M)
> Build completed
> Verifying instantiation in sfo1
> [0] 6-3-e2e-tests@1.0.0 now-start /home/nowuser/src
> [0] npm run server
> [0] 6-3-e2e-tests@1.0.0 server /home/nowuser/src
> [0] next start
> [1] 6-3-e2e-tests@1.0.0 now-start /home/nowuser/src
> [1] npm run server
> [1] 6-3-e2e-tests@1.0.0 server /home/nowuser/src
> [1] next start
> [2] 6-3-e2e-tests@1.0.0 now-start /home/nowuser/src
> [2] npm run server
> Scaled 1 instance in sfo1 [26s]
> Success! Deployment ready
```

Just copy-paste the address, `https://whatever-been-assigned.now.sh`, and observe your website in the wild.

Now, let's automate the deployment using Travis, because right now we only can deploy from the local dev computer.

In order to deploy, we will need a `Now.sh` token; you can copy-paste it from `~/.now/auth.json` and it look like this:

```
// ~/.now/auth.json
{
  "_": "This is your Now credentials file. DON'T SHARE! More:
https://git.io/v5ECz",
  "credentials": [
    {
      "provider": "sh",
      "token": "xxxxxxxxxxxxxxxxxxxxxxx"
    }
  ]
}
```

Go to `http://travis-ci.org` and open your repository settings there, paste the token in the *Environment Variables* section and make sure **Display value in logs** is `OFF`.

We will need a package from npm:

```
$ npm install now --save-dev
```

Alter .travis.yml to make use of the installed package:

```
# .travis.yml
language: node_js
node_js:
- stable
after_success:
- npm run now-deploy
```

Add the script to `package.json`:

```
// package.json
{
 "scripts": {
    "build": "next build",
    "now-deploy": "now -e NODE_ENV=production --token $NOW_TOKEN --npm --
public",
    "now-start": "next start",
    "start": "next",
    "test": "NODE_ENV=test jest"
  }
}
```

Commit, push, wait, and see the logs in TravisCI; the address of the deployment is there, the same way as in the local deployment. You probably would want to also add `alias` for your website at `Now.sh`, as this will allow you to expose your website via a custom domain.

Psst! Docker deployments are also supported; just put a `Dockerfile` in your Git repository.

Summary

In this chapter, we finalized our knowledge of Next.js, and now we can deploy the app in various different ways to many different services, we have learned how to create a service-independent deployment container.

This means that now, you as a developer can create a full-stack app that will follow all these best practices:

- Server-side rendering
- APIs
- SEO-friendly routing
- Beautiful styles
- Authentication
- Role-based access control
- Logging
- Analytics
- Tests
- E2E tests
- Continuous integration with coverage tracking
- Containerized deployment

From now on, your apps will be absolutely awesome with such a stack of goodies.

Hope it was fun reading this book, best wishes!

Other Books You May Enjoy

If you enjoyed this book, you may be interested in these other books by Packt:

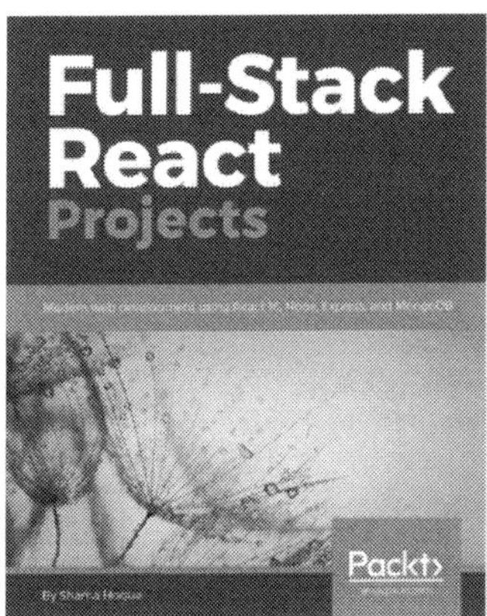

Full-Stack React Projects
Shama Hoque

ISBN: 978-1-78883-553-4

- Set up your development environment and develop a MERN application
- Implement user authentication and authorization using JSON Web Tokens
- Build a social media application by extending the basic MERN application
- Create an online marketplace application with shopping cart and Stripe payments
- Develop a media streaming application using MongoDB GridFS
- Implement server-side rendering with data to improve SEO
- Set up and use React 360 to develop user interfaces with VR capabilities
- Learn industry best practices to make MERN stack applications reliable and scalable

React: Cross-Platform Application Development with React Native
Emilio Rodriguez Martinez

ISBN: 978-1-78913-608-1

- Structure React Native projects to ease maintenance and extensibility
- Optimize a project to speed up development
- Use external modules to speed up the development and maintenance of your projects
- Explore the different UI and code patterns to be used for iOS and Android
- Get to know the best practices when building apps in React Native

Leave a review - let other readers know what you think

Please share your thoughts on this book with others by leaving a review on the site that you bought it from. If you purchased the book from Amazon, please leave us an honest review on this book's Amazon page. This is vital so that other potential readers can see and use your unbiased opinion to make purchasing decisions, we can understand what our customers think about our products, and our authors can see your feedback on the title that they have worked with Packt to create. It will only take a few minutes of your time, but is valuable to other potential customers, our authors, and Packt. Thank you!

Index

Made in the USA
Middletown, DE
17 July 2021